DINNER ● ONE TAKE

Quarto.com

© 2024 Quarto Publishing Group USA Inc.
Text © 2024 Emeus Corley

First Published in 2024 by The Harvard Common Press, an imprint of The Quarto Group,
100 Cummings Center, Suite 265-D, Beverly, MA 01915, USA.
T (978) 282-9590 F (978) 283-2742

The Harvard Common Press titles are also available at discount for retail, wholesale,
promotional, and bulk purchase. For details, contact the Special Sales Manager by email
at specialsales@quarto.com or by mail at The Quarto Group, Attn: Special Sales Manager,
100 Cummings Center, Suite 265-D, Beverly, MA 01915, USA.

28 27 26 25 24   1 2 3 4 5

ISBN: 978-0-7603-8737-5

Digital edition published in 2024
eISBN: 978-0-7603-8738-2

Library of Congress Cataloging-in-Publication Data available.

Design & Page layout: Justin Page
Cover Images: Photography by Kelsey Foster (Front cover: top right, bottom center,
    bottom left) and Zack Bowen (Front cover: top left, bottom right, center left;
    Back cover: all); Food styling by Sheila James (Front cover: top left, bottom right,
    center left; Back cover: all)
Photography: Kelsey Foster (pages 7, 8, 12, 15, 19, 23, 27, 30, 36–37, 52, 55, 57, 59, 62–63,
    66, 84, 85, 87, 92, 105, 107, 114, 115, 121, 131, 133, 139, 151, 157, 166, 169, 170, 173,
    175, 179, 189), Zack Bowen (pages 4, 33, 43, 47, 49, 69, 73, 77, 78–79, 83, 89, 97, 99, 100,
    109, 111, 118, 123, 125, 128–129, 137, 142, 147, 154–155, 163, 181, 183, 184, 185), and
    Shutterstock (pages 21, 25, 38, 70, 95, 102, 149, 159)
Food Styling: Sheila James (pages 4, 33, 43, 47, 49, 69, 73, 77, 78–79, 83, 89, 97, 99, 100, 109,
    111, 118, 123, 125, 128–129, 137, 142, 147, 154–155, 163, 181, 183, 184, 185)

Printed in China

DINNER IN ONE TAKE

WEEKNIGHT-FRIENDLY MEALS THAT ARE BIG ON FLAVOR, NOT TIME

BO CORLEY

HARVARD COMMON PRESS

Contents

Introduction

A lot of people start their cooking journey with recipes. Although recipes are an important part of cooking, they are just a part: To me, cooking is about the connections among recipes, techniques, history, and stories. In this book, I want you to join me for all of this. I hope you not only enjoy the recipes but understand more about the *why* behind specific ingredients or the *history* of a recipe. Recipes aside, I hope this book will serve as a resource that you can refer back to—and something that will help you become a more informed grocery shopper as well!

WHERE I'M COMING FROM

When I was a kid, before social media, there was the Food Network. While my friends were out riding bikes, I was inside watching Emeril. I still remember yelling "Bam" in the kitchen and that feeling of "making food happy." Eventually, when my parents would return from the grocery store with groceries for the week, I started treating it like a challenge. I looked at that bounty and planned an epic meal!

Fast-forward to my adult life and I had lost that connection to cooking, though I still ate plenty of tasty food. I had a decade-long career in the corporate space, which meant a lot of eating out, catered lunches, and entertaining clients over meals. This was part of what was, ultimately, a successful career, but my health declined. Eating out was the most convenient option. I would spend time with my kids when I got home and then it was back to work bright and early. No excuses, though: I had no discipline and was not taking care of myself. At my heaviest, I weighed 475 pounds (215 kg).

Funny enough, my weight-loss journey and my rediscovery of cooking started back at my childhood home. I remember flying back to Cleveland to see my mom for Mother's Day and she had lost quite a bit of weight. She inspired me to start my own exercise and weight-loss journey. I quickly realized what you put into your body is as important as working out. Still, I loved great-tasting food and I refused to fully restrict myself. How could I stay true to cooking all types of food but live a healthier lifestyle? That was the challenge I took on over the next few years.

I'm happy to say I did lose more than 200 pounds (91 kg) over time by taking a realistic approach to my nutrition. A big portion of my weight loss was understanding labels in the grocery store, as well as what was good and bad for *my* body. (I love that idea, too, that my body is different from everyone else's. There is no cookie-cutter diet that everyone should follow.)

THE MEAL PREP YEARS

Okay, so while I was losing that weight, I was still working in corporate America. That means prep became a big part of my life. At first, one of the things that bothered me was that flavor and juiciness often suffered when I meal prepped because I was reheating things—cooking things twice. I started paying attention and learning things like by smoking chicken low and slow you get better (juicier) reheated chicken. Instead of cooking rice according to the directions, add extra water to be cooked off when reheating. Over time, I developed all sorts of tricks and tidbits that made for, what I call, "proper prep."

After I lost the weight and the pandemic hit, I started sharing what I learned with a broader community. Remember, this is the time when nurses, first responders, and others were flat out. By the time they got to the grocery store, they were out of energy and the stores were sometimes out of key ingredients. When I first launched my meal prep company, I focused on helping first responders and the elderly. Over time, Proper Prep took all clients, including professional body-builders. In doing that, I had to dive even further into nutrition and different client requirements. I started building a mental library of information that changed the way I cooked. It was a clean approach to not-so-clean food.

THIS BOOK

So, how does all this relate to what you see on my channels and in this book? Really, where my food philosophy landed is all about balance and attention to detail. These days, when I come up with a recipe, it's not just "oil, salt, and pepper," but picking my favorite specific type of each. Ingredients matter. The pans you cook in matter. Seasonings matter. The quality of meat matters. I want people to read this book and cook my recipes and realize that if you just pay a *little* more attention, you can become a better cook. Once you understand how to make small changes, even in existing recipes, you will get more flavorful, elevated cooking.

The recipes in this book also speak to my current inspiration, day in and day out: getting dinner on the table for my family. I was an only child. We always sat down together and ate dinner. So, when I had kids, I wanted to duplicate that same process, but for years I just wasn't able to. Once I started, however, I gave it my all and tried to make up for lost time. The recipes in this book speak to the way that my family, and most families, tend to go through the week. They are greatest-hits recipes that are not complicated to make. Here are some common snapshots of how I use them:

- When everyone's out all day and not back until evening—and maybe the kids aren't even all back at the same time—for dinner, go for Endless Pizza (page 127) or Top-Tier Toasted Sandos (page 126).

- With four kids, choosing your own adventure is important, too. If you have a bunch of people to feed with different tastes, Family Night (or Game Day) Quesadillas (page 42) to the rescue.

- With my son playing football, sometimes I have to feed more around the table—doubly challenging for picky teenagers. Steak for a Crowd (page 40) it is.

- Date night with your partner is also important. Sometimes, you have a free evening and you don't want to go out to eat. That's why I include a couple of fancy recipes, like the Shrimp Un-Tacos (page 124) and A5 + Egg (page 46).

- Unexpected guests or a happy hour with the neighbors? Check out The Beverage Lab and Perfect Bites chapters!

- Weekday breakfast doesn't always happen, so why not have that breakfast for dinner? Whip up a Come to the Table Potato Skillet (page 96) or Cloud Eggs (page 106) to scratch that itch.

- Weekends that are more relaxed are for celebrating the smoker—hang out by the smoker or grill and make that Proper Pulled Pork (see page 50), Three-for-One Spareribs (page 61), or Texas Brisket with a Twist (page 54).

No matter your family size, the recipe you choose, or the week's schedule, the key is cooking some dinners at home. Cooking is a love language. The person preparing the food is showing love when they prepare and serve it, and there's community in the household when everyone comes together. It just hits differently than picking up the delivery bag from the porch.

GUESS THE MEAL

My oldest would often try to guess what I was cooking for dinner. He got pretty good, so I started throwing him curveballs. I pick up a pork shoulder for the weekend and put it on the counter, but he thought it was for that night . . . nope, pizza.

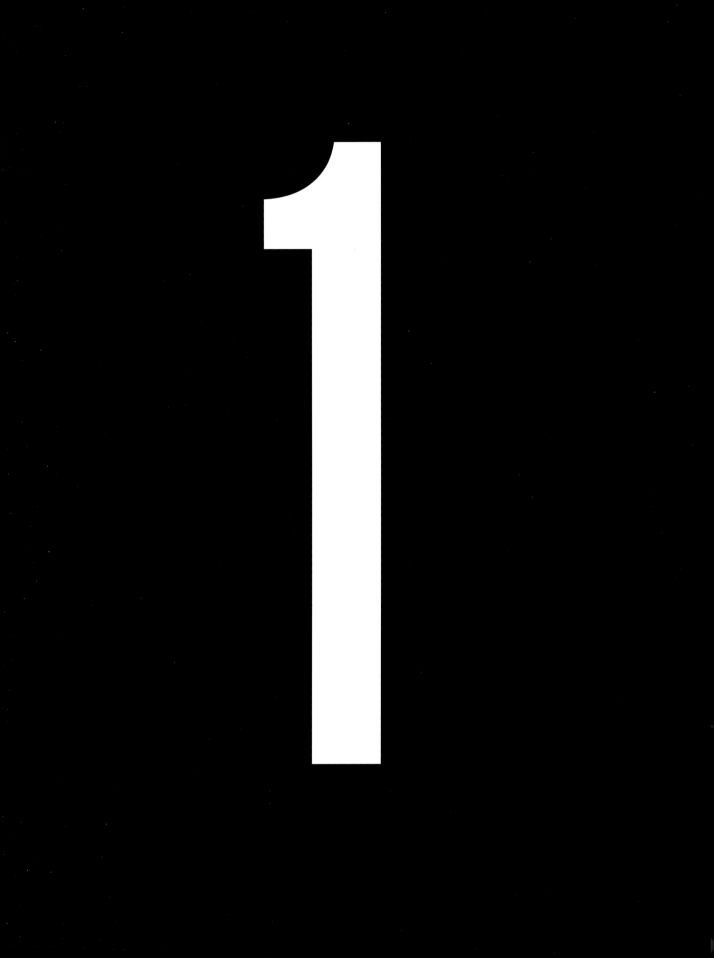

Bo's Blueprints

Knowing when to use a stainless steel pan vs. nonstick, or low smoke–point vs. high smoke–point oils, for example, is a great first step. Then, go further: I use avocado oil instead of seed oils for high temperatures, for example, because of its high smoke point. Although you don't have to do exactly what I do, my hope is that this chapter will prepare you to successfully recreate the dishes in the following chapters. Let's get set up for success.

MY KITCHEN TOOLS

You don't have to spend a ton of money to get great kitchen tools these days (though I admit, it is fun to spend some money on great tools as well!). My general advice is to buy the best quality you can afford for the workhorse tools before you splurge on specialty items. A great knife and cutting board are worth so much more than a stand mixer for day-in and day-out cooking.

KNIVES

When it comes to picking a knife, here's the thing: Think about how you use knives and how that relates to hardness. Have you heard of the Rockwell Hardness Scale? It's how you can tell softer metals from harder ones. Stick with me …

If you are a heavy chopper, like when you're chopping cilantro it sounds like you're chopping wood, go with a rating of 60 steel chef's knife. The shape of the knife will give you a good rocking motion and the harder steel means you won't need to sharpen it as often. Now, if you are a slicer, mostly going knife tip on board, you can go for a softer blade, in the 100 to 110 rating range. Also, generally speaking, if you're a person with a lot of experience, and you've used a lot of knives, I recommend a softer metal.

CUTTING BOARDS

Wood

My personal preference for my main cutting board, the one I use the most, is a teakwood cutting board. It's soft when it's seasoned properly, and because I use a lot of high-end knives, it helps extend the life of my knives. I don't believe in glass or metal as a main option for a cutting board. They dull knives. In fact, even hard plastic can dull knives faster than wood.

Season it: Because wood is porous, it will dry out. If there's a crack in your cutting board, it will jeopardize its integrity. To keep a wooden cutting board moisturized, I recommend using wood cutting board–specific oils; I tend to use food-grade mineral oil to rub down the board. I do it once every couple of weeks—though, keep in mind, I cook a lot. Keep an eye on your board. If it's dry, add some oil.

> **CHEAT CODE: W**ash an oiled wooden cutting board with soap and water but never let it air-dry. Wipe it dry with a microfiber cloth and stand it up to let any residual moisture evaporate.

GET SHARP

If you've never purchased a knife, I'd recommend a 9- to 10-inch (23 to 25 cm) chef's knife as your first purchase for versatility, and a utility knife to get into smaller places (or to use in place of a paring knife). My third favorite knife is a santoku because I eat a lot of potatoes and onions, which are full of moisture. A santoku knife has serrations on the blade, giving you air between the knife and what you're cutting and so it won't stick to the food—whereas a chef's knife, without the serrations, will stick. But think about what you cook the most and buy your third knife—a.k.a. your first more specialized knife—based on what your first two knives are not doing well enough.

Plastic

Now, there are times when I don't use my wooden board. Wood is porous, so for raw chicken, fish, red meat, etc., I use a plastic cutting board (the famous white board from my videos) to prevent contaminating the board. Can you cut meat on a wood cutting board? Yes, you can, but I don't recommend it. Think of how you season a wood cutting board with oil. Because of its porous nature, the oil can soak into the wood. Unless you're going to immediately take the board, wash it off with soapy water, and disinfect it with vinegar after using it to cut raw meat, I recommend a plastic cutting board instead. Also, it may be obvious, but do not cut cooked meat on the same cutting board that you cut raw meat on.

Store It Right

I went through a period of trying everything to see how it impacted storing food, including aluminum foil, plastic wrap, and various types of containers. When it comes to fruit, vegetables, and even meat (except in rare situations), I found the best way to preserve flavor and freshness is with an airtight container. My go-to options are glass reusable storage containers with a tight-fitting lid or glass Mason jars. Bonus: You can also quickly see what's inside them.

PANS

Whether I grab cast iron, stainless, or nonstick is largely a temperature conversation. First let's talk about cast iron.

A cast-iron pan is going to hold the highest temperature. From a heat perspective, if you're going high heat, searing, and, in some cases, frying, I recommend cast iron or stainless steel. I find these materials the most forgiving. From a safety perspective, however, you do have to be careful as the entire pan gets hot, and they can be heavy. My cast-iron pans are my go-to pans for steak, potatoes, and anything going stovetop to oven (you can do this with stainless, but I never do).

Stainless steel can be used for searing. Although I prefer cast iron for steak, I use stainless whenever I cook fish or eggs (especially fried, crispy eggs), and to sauté veggies. Using stainless successfully can take some practice. Here's my tip: The Leidenfrost test is a phenomenon that says that when the surface you're heating hits a certain temperature, it creates a water vapor layer between the hot surface and the item you're cooking. If you put water droplets in a hot pan and they do not evaporate, but dance, your pan is the perfect temperature. If they don't dance, the pan is not hot enough. If they evaporate, it's too hot.

A nonstick pan, in my opinion, should not be heated to more than 325°F (163°C). If it is, you run the risk of releasing metals from the nonstick coating into your food. So, nonstick is a low-heat pan for me—scrambling eggs, making an omelet, slow-roasting veggies, cooking smothered chicken, or other low-temp baked dishes.

A Note on Aprons

Okay, so I had a bad kitchen accident and burned myself. From that day forward, I like leather aprons. They protect you well from burns and they also clean up well. I clean mine with soap and water once a week, and I'm done. Plus, they make me feel like a Viking. Now, I also recommend an apron with pockets, because you'll find all sorts of times you'll want to keep your tools handy.

OTHER GENERAL SAFETY TIPS

- Lay meat away from you when placing it in a pan or hot oil.
- Never leave anything unattended when cooking. With advances in technology, it's easy to think you can walk away from a grill or smoker, but you should never leave a cook because you never know what can happen—and I have experienced this personally.
- Take every safety precaution necessary.

SEASONINGS AND OILS

One of the most important aspects of cooking is the ingredients you use—and this means all ingredients. No matter how good your meat and veggies are, what you cook them in and season them with is just as important, if not more. You can ruin a great piece of meat with bad oil and seasoning.

SALT, PEPPER, SPG

Salt
Kosher salt is my standard, and is what I use in all recipes unless specified otherwise. I try to stay away from iodized salt. I've just found, in some situations, it gives you an off-putting flavor. My other go-tos are flaky salt and pink Himalayan, which I find a little sweeter. For example, after I've sliced a steak and am plating, I'll often use pink Himalayan to add the finishing touch.

Black Pepper
I've found that if you cook pepper past 325°F (163°C), some varieties get bitter. I like Tellicherry pepper because it avoids this and has a more complex pepper flavor. In some situations, I also like pink peppercorns, but Tellicherry is my go-to. My recipes call for freshly ground black pepper, so you can use your favorite.

SPG
I love SPG, a.k.a. a 1:1:1 ratio of salt, pepper, and garlic powder. My mix uses kosher salt, Tellicherry peppercorns, and granulated garlic.

OILS

Whatever oil you pick should be selected based primarily on whatever temperature you're going for. Different people have different preferences, but here are my picks:

High Heat
Avocado oil, which I think is cleanest from both production and taste standpoints and it has a high smoke point.

Low Heat
Extra-virgin olive oil that is cold pressed or expeller pressed guarantees no additives.

Deep-Frying
Peanut oil can handle high heat without leaving a burned flavor on the outside of your food. Sometimes, when you deep-fry in avocado oil, it just feel as though the food cooks on the outside a little too fast, without fully cooking inside.

BO'S GOLD

Use this in a recipe instead of unflavored oil for a flavor boost, or drizzle this oil over pizza for an extra pop of flavor.

1 teaspoon **red pepper flakes**
1 teaspoon **black sesame seeds**
2 large **cinnamon sticks**
1 teaspoon **whole cloves**
3 **garlic cloves**, peeled
1 **shallot**, peeled
3 **bay leaves**
1 bunch fresh **curly-leaf parsley**, used whole
1 cup (240 ml) **avocado oil**

Makes about 1 cup (240 ml)

In a medium-size saucepan over medium-low heat, combine all the ingredients. Cook for 20 minutes. Remove from the heat and let cool for 30 minutes. Pour the liquid through a fine-mesh strainer into a medium-size bowl. Using a funnel, transfer the oil, which should be an amber–dark gold color, to a small glass container with a tight-fitting lid and keep in an airtight container for up to 2 weeks.

NONSTICK COOKING SPRAY

I will use EVOO spray that is expeller pressed, but many times I just make my own. As long as you have flour, oil, and butter, you can, too.

½ cup (120 ml) **avocado oil**
½ cup (120 ml) **melted butter**
½ cup (60 g) **all-purpose flour**

Makes about 1 cup (240 ml)

In a medium-size bowl, whisk together all the ingredients. Transfer to a spray bottle. Use immediately or store in the refrigerator for up to 2 weeks.

KNOW YOUR BUTTERS

Butter comes in all sorts of varieties, from whipped to European. These days, you can even find avocado oil–based and oat milk–based butters.

American butter is required by law to contain a minimum of 80 percent butterfat. That's right, this is a minimum, so some U.S. butter has more fat than other U.S. butter! European and Irish butters typically contain 82 to 85 percent butterfat and are also usually churned longer. The grass in Ireland is high in beta-carotene and the grass-fed cows eat that grass—that's why you get that gold color in butter made from their milk. Amish butter is anywhere between 84 and 85 percent butterfat.

Butter is composed of three main ingredients: butterfat, water, and milk solids. Ghee is butter without the milk solids and water. Ghee is expensive in the grocery store, but you can make it at home: You're clarifying your butter, so you'll want to put a few sticks of butter in a medium-size saucepan over low heat. You're ultimately trying to create three layers: a foamy layer on top, a layer on the bottom, and a middle layer that is liquid gold clarified butter. Once you have three layers, remove the pan from the heat and let the melted butter cool for 5 minutes. Place a coffee filter over a pint-size (480 ml) Mason jar, securing it with a rubber band. Pour the melted butter through the filter. Store your clarified butter in a cool, dark place or your refrigerator and use within a month.

BO'S BROWNED BUTTER

If you want a rich, elevated butter that has a little bit of a nutty flavor, you definitely have to try browned butter. Think about eating a regular cashew and then eating a honey-roasted cashew. That's what it's like.

1 cup (2 sticks, or 226 g) **butter**

Makes about ¾ cup (156 g)

In a small saucepan over low heat, melt the butter while stirring continuously. You want those milk solids to brown, not burn. After about 4 to 5 minutes, once the butter is browned to a golden croissant-like hue, pour it into an airtight container and scoop off any foam. You should have a much richer, amber color with that browned butter compared with regular butter and ghee. Keep in the refrigerator for up to a month or on the kitchen counter at room temperature for up to 2 weeks.

TALLOW

When you trim brisket, pulled pork, or steak, don't discard the excess fat. You can cook it on the stovetop over low heat for 2 hours—my preferred method is to put it in an oven-safe container and let it cook and render down while you smoke your meats. Store in an airtight container or jar for up to 2 weeks in the refrigerator.

CARAMELIZED SHALLOT BUTTER

Let's talk about the shallot. It's part of the allium family, so it's in the same family as leeks, garlic, and other onions. Shallots are typically sweeter and more subtly flavored than other onions. Shallots are my favorite onions, and this is my favorite thing to make with them.

Avocado oil cooking spray
½ cup (80 g) diced **shallot**
¼ cup (60 ml) **red wine vinegar**
¼ cup (60 g) packed **dark brown sugar**
½ cup (1 stick, or 113 g) **butter**, cubed, at room temperature
2 teaspoons **dried tarragon**

Makes about ½ cup (130 g)

1. Heat a medium-size skillet over medium-high heat, then spray the skillet with a light coating of avocado oil. Reduce the heat to medium-low and add the shallots to the skillet. Sauté for about 2 minutes until translucent. Add the vinegar and dark brown sugar. Cook, stirring often, until your mixture is a dark golden brown with a smooth consistency, 5 to 7 minutes. Remove the skillet from the heat and let cool for 5 to 10 minutes.

2. Meanwhile, in a small mixing bowl, combine the butter and tarragon. Use a hand mixer to whip the butter on a low speed for 1 to 2 minutes. Increase the speed to high and beat for about 1 minute until the butter is fluffy. Take those caramelized onions from your skillet and fold them into the whipped butter. Keep the butter refrigerated in an airtight container for up to 2 weeks.

3. The beauty of this recipe is if the "tang is tanging" too much, dial back the vinegar and add some more sugar. If it's too sweet, do the opposite. I use this butter when I'm roasting or sautéing vegetables, buttering buns for burgers, and even as a topper for salmon.

GARLIC 3 WAYS: OIL, ROASTED, CONFIT BUTTER

Here are three ways to use up large amounts of garlic quickly because I can't be the only person who buys garlic in bulk and then a week later I'm like, "What the heck am I about to do with all of this garlic?"

1 cup (136 g) peeled **garlic cloves**
1 cup (240 ml) **avocado oil**
1 teaspoon **kosher salt**
1 **rosemary sprig**
1 tablespoon (2.5 g) chopped **fresh sage**
½ cup (1 stick, or 113 g) **butter**, at room temperature

1. Preheat the oven to 400°F (204°C).

2. Place the whole garlic cloves in an oven-safe ramekin. Pour the oil over the garlic and sprinkle with the salt. Use scissors to cut the rosemary sprig into 3 sections and add them to the ramekin. Since we're putting the ramekin in the oven, I suggest putting it on a baking sheet first and then into the oven. Removing a ramekin full of bubbling, hot oil from the oven is risky business, and the baking sheet will protect you from burns and spills.

3. Bake for 1 hour 15 minutes or so until the garlic is a dark golden color on top. Carefully remove the ramekin from the oven and let cool for 30 minutes to 1 hour.

4. Place a fine-mesh strainer over a large bowl.

5. To make garlic oil, separate the oil from the garlic by putting it through the strainer set over the bowl. You'll keep both the oil and the garlic. Transfer the oil to a small glass jar or cruet. I like to place the empty jar in my clean sink and use a funnel to transfer the oil from the bowl to the jar. You've now made your first finished product—garlic oil. When stored in the refrigerator, this oil will keep for 3 to 5 days. I use mine when I'm roasting tomatoes, making sauces, and especially when I'm making garlic bread.

6. Our next two products use the reserved roasted garlic cloves.

7. To make roasted garlic, when you strained out the oil, your strainer should have caught all of the whole garlic cloves. If you'd like to use the cloves as is, you can use them now or store them in an airtight container in the refrigerator for 3 to 5 days (like your oil). When you're look- ing for extra razzle-dazzle in your homemade dressings and sauces, roasted garlic cloves are the way to go.

8. To make garlic confit butter, if you'd like, place the roasted cloves in a medium-size bowl and use a fork to mash them until you have a paste. Add the sage and butter to the bowl and use the fork to mash and combine the in- gredients. You now have garlic confit butter, which you can spread on bread, stir into potatoes, or even slather over a Cornish hen before roasting.

EASY ROASTED GARLIC

Okay, so there is a fourth garlic recipe here as well, but sometimes you need to make roasted garlic on the fly. I like this method as you don't even need to peel before roasting.

2 heads garlic
1½ teaspoons **olive oil**

1. Preheat the oven to 400°F (204°C).

2. Cut the tops off the garlic heads to expose the cloves and place them on a square of aluminum foil (you can loosely wrap with foil, but don't wrap tightly or cover). Drizzle with the olive oil. Roast for 30 to 40 minutes until soft and golden brown. When done, the garlic cloves should easily squeeze out of their skins when pressed. If you're making a day or three ahead of time, just pop the cloves into a small glass container with a tight-fitting lid and store in the fridge.

SMOKING

Although pellet grills are sometimes frowned upon in the barbecue community, if you are a novice or expert, so much of the technology that's out now provides a more convenient and inexpensive way to produce good, smoked meat. At the time of writing, I have everything from an old-school vertical wood-fueled smoker to a 48-inch (120 cm) pellet grill. My favorite grill to use is powered by pellets, but you can also put lump wood in it when you need to. If I'm cooking brisket, pulled pork, really anything big but not long, I use a vertical smoker—but you don't *need* to do that yourself. All the recipes in this book are pellet grill friendly as long as you can find a way to work in wood chunks for extra flavor. If your grill or smoker doesn't have a way to utilize wood chunks, there are tools you can buy to get wood into the mix—a smoking tube, for example—and I recommend looking into it.

CHEAT CODE: If you are shopping for a smoker, make sure to find one with a great seal around the edges.

Now, time for some controversy:

Opinion #1:
Some people swear by the idea of clean smoke and dirty smoke—meaning, there's a period of time while the initial pellets or wood burn when people don't cook. Here's my take: Once my smoker gets to temperature, I put what I'm cooking in it. It's damn near impossible to get clear smoke on a pellet grill or digital system, and anything harsh burning off will have done so by the time you hit temperature.

Opinion #2:
I may get some flak for this, but I believe post oak is a good wood, not the only wood, to use when smoking. I like it as a wood to turn to when you start off, for sure, as it burns superhot and has a well-balanced flavor. But once you establish successful fire maintenance and temperature control, I strongly encourage you to experiment with at least peach, hickory, and mesquite woods. Try different combos of wood. For beef, oak and mesquite are an awesome combo. For pork, peach complements the fatty flesh, giving a sweet but smoky flavor. The combinations are endless, and I rarely smoke with just one type of wood.

TEMPERATURE PROBES

I am a huge fan of technology in the kitchen and when smoking. If there is one kitchen tool/gadget I think everyone should have, it's a temperature probe. I personally prefer the Typhur brand, but there are several options on the market.

Ambient temperature is the temperature inside your smoker/grill/oven, and you need to pay attention to that in addition to your internal meat temperature because different areas of your grill or smoker may burn at different temps. For example, if you set your grill to 250°F (121°C), the ambient temperature of the air around whatever meat you're cooking might be lower depending on which rack or position in the grill (smoker, oven) you place your meat.

If you don't have a thermometer yet, an easy hot zone test is to place several uncooked biscuits in all areas of your grill. Preheat the grill to hold a temperature of about 350°F (180°C) first. After 10 minutes (or as long as you want to cook them), you will notice some biscuits are cooking faster and are more well done than others. These biscuits identify your "hot zones." I often do this when I get a new grill. Since you have to throw out anything in the initial burn out/break in, it's a great time to learn—even if you waste a few biscuits.

Meat at My House

It used to be every Wednesday that my boys would bring beverages and I would provide the barbecue. It gave us time to decompress, and we probably didn't even realize it at the time. After moving to Texas, and as the kids got older and schedules got busier, proper barbecue became something that moved more toward the weekend. No matter what day or night you're looking to smoke, grill, or sear, this chapter has some of my favorites.

SUPER SOUS VIDE BURGERS

Sous vide may seem intimidating, but it's one of the most foolproof ways to get meat to render down. Most people who get into sous vide cooking go right for steaks and seafood. That's great, but don't sleep on things like burgers. Why? Well, think about it: A burger is normally ground chuck. That intramuscular fat, when you put it in sous vide, renders extremely slowly. And with sous vide, it doesn't all drip out of the burger.

LET'S TALK TEXTURE

But wait, what about texture? Don't worry. I'm a huge smash burger fan and admit that you just don't get that same crust when you cook using the sous vide method. The good news is that you can undershoot your final temp and add it back at the end of the process with a quick sear in a cast-iron pan. It's pretty much a reverse sear (see page 35). Want to take it to the next level? Make your own Backyard Burger Buns (page 34), or try swapping regular butter for my Caramelized Shallot Butter (page 22) when you're toasting your buns.

2 pounds (908 g) **lean ground beef**
½ teaspoon **kosher salt**
1 tablespoon (6 g) freshly ground **black pepper**
1 **garlic clove**, thinly sliced
4 **rosemary sprigs**
2 tablespoons (30 ml) **Bo's Gold** (page 18), **avocado oil**, or olive oil
4 **slices cheddar cheese**
4 tablespoons (½ stick, or 56 g) **butter**
4 hamburger buns or **Backyard Burger Buns** (page 34)
1 cup (250 g) **barbecue sauce**
2 teaspoons **dried tarragon**
4 **Little Gem lettuce leaves**

Serves 4

1. Start by taking your ground beef and dividing and rolling it into four balls. They should be a good size, since uncooked they will be about 8 ounces (225 g) each. Flatten the balls using parchment paper and your hands and season with salt and pepper.

2. Put each patty into its own vacuum-sealable bag. Add a few slices of garlic to one side of each patty and a rosemary sprig to the other side of each patty. Seal the bags.

3. Set up your sous vide. Preheat a water bath to 155°F (68°C) using a sous vide immersion circulator. Insert the burgers and cook for 1½ to 2 hours.

4. Once the burgers are done in the sous vide, heat a large skillet over medium-high heat. Remove the patties from the bags, leaving the rosemary and garlic in the bags. Drizzle Bo's Gold in the hot skillet and add the patties. Brown the patties by searing for up to 2 minutes per side, or until the patties are close to your desired temperature. When the burgers are almost done cooking, place a slice of cheddar on each to melt. Remove the burgers from the skillet once the cheese has melted.

5. Heat a large, clean skillet over medium-high heat. Add the butter to the skillet to melt and swirl to coat the pan. Toast the insides of your buns in the skillet until golden, 2 to 3 minutes.

6. To assemble, spread ¼ cup (62.5 g) of barbecue sauce on the toasted side of each top bun. Place a patty on each bottom bun, sprinkle with tarragon, top with lettuce, and close the burger with the top bun.

BACKYARD BURGER BUNS

I'm not the type to bake every day, or even every week. But when I have the time, I love making my own burger buns. Most breads you buy in the store have some level of preservatives to keep them soft. Maybe your local bakery has good sourdough without all that stuff. But what are the chances they make burger buns? Around me, it's just not that common. And that's a shame because fresh buns can really elevate a burger.

1 cup (240 ml) **water**

¼ cup (50 g) **sugar**

2 (0.25-ounce, or 7 g) packets **active dry yeast**

⅓ cup (80 ml) **avocado oil**

1 cup (120 g) **all-purpose flour,** divided, plus more for rolling

1 **large egg yolk**

1 teaspoon **milk**

2 tablespoons (16 g) **sesame seeds**

Makes 4 buns

1. In a small saucepan over medium-low heat, heat the water to no hotter than 110°F (43°C). Transfer to a large mixing bowl and add the sugar, yeast, and oil. Stir and let sit for 5 to 10 minutes to activate the yeast.

2. Add ½ cup (60 g) of flour to the yeast mixture. Using a handheld or a stand mixer fitted with the paddle attachment, mix for 1 minute on low speed to combine. Slowly sprinkle in the remaining ½ cup (60 g) flour while keeping the mixer on low speed. Once the ingredients are combined, turn off the mixer, cover the bowl with a microfiber towel, and let rise for 1 to 2 hours until the dough doubles in size.

3. Line a baking sheet with parchment paper.

4. Lightly dust a work surface with flour and transfer the dough to it. Divide the dough into eight equal portions. Gently roll each portion into a ball and place on the prepared baking sheet.

5. Preheat the oven to 400°F (204°C).

6. In a small bowl, use a fork to whisk the egg and milk. Brush each dough ball with the egg mixture and top with sesame seeds.

7. Bake for about 15 minutes until the outside is golden brown. Let rest and enjoy!

REVERSE SEAR RIB EYES

4 (1-pound, or 454 g) **rib-eye steaks**
1 tablespoon (18 g) **flaky salt**
2 tablespoons (24 g) **SPG** (see page 17)
2 tablespoons (32 g) **Caramelized Shallot Butter** (page 22)

Serves 4

I love a good rib eye. When you have a great cut of steak, all you really need to make it tasty is salt, pepper, and garlic. If you can't get your hands on a good rib eye, this recipe works well for any fatty cut of steak (porterhouse, bone-in New York strip, T-bone).

My preferred method to cook steaks like these is reverse searing because it allows you to get the exact temperature you're going for. The general rule is you pull the steak 12°F (7°C) colder than the final temp, then sear it to your desired temp. The initial slow cook allows the fat, especially the fat cap on a rib eye, to render. When you combine that rendered fat with a hard char from a sear, it's just the best bite. You'll need wood or pellets of choice for smoking (I use mostly mesquite for this recipe).

1. Place a wire rack on a sheet pan. Pat the steaks dry with a paper towel. Sprinkle with the salt and transfer to the fridge to rest, uncovered, for 12 to 24 hours.

2. Remove the steaks from the fridge and pat dry.

CHEAT CODE: Patting the steaks dry is important. It will remove some of the salt and the moisture that will get in the way of the sear.

3. Cover both sides of the steaks and the fat cap with SPG.

4. Preheat the smoker to 215°F (102°C) and add your wood to the wood box.

5. Add the steaks to the smoker and let them go until they reach an internal temperature of about 110°F (43°C). Time will vary based on your equipment and conditions but should be a little less than 1 hour.

6. Preheat a large cast-iron skillet over medium-high heat.

7. Place the steaks and butter in the skillet (you will need to work in batches) and sear for 1 to 2 minutes until a nice crust forms and the steaks reach your desired doneness temp (I aim for 145°F [63°C], which is a nice solid medium, usually). Let your steaks rest for 5 to 10 minutes before serving.

REVERSE SEAR CHICKEN, TOO!

Usually, when you talk about reverse searing, it's all about red meat and steak. But, if you apply this process to chicken, you can get a juicy piece of meat every time as well. I'm going to teach you three different ways to do a reverse sear with chicken breasts:

The cook:

Method 1. Smoke the chicken on a smoker or grill at 250°F (121°C) until the target internal temperature of 163°F (73°C).

Method 2. Sous vide: Cook at 145°F (63°C) until the chicken hits the desired internal temperature.

Method 3. Preheat the oven to 250°F (121°C). Cook the chicken until it hits 163°F (73°C).

The sear:

If you go smoke or grill (method 1), stay on theme. Crank up the heat to high and, once the grates are good and hot, go ahead and get some nice grill marks on the chicken for the sear, and you'll be good to go. If you're going with sous vide (method 2) or oven (method 3), I recommend pan-searing with avocado oil at a high temperature until you get a nice crust.

SMASH BURGERS

What's a cookbook these days without a smash burger recipe? Unlike some of the other recipes in this book, this one is for those times when you want to indulge and enjoy. After making a variety of smash burgers, I figured out a couple cheat codes to make a burger that tastes good by design even better. The first tip is to combine Italian sausage with fatty ground beef. It makes for a flavorful and super juicy patty. Second, be sure to add the bacon grease as instructed. This will take your sear up another level.

2 pounds (908 g) 80/20 **ground beef**
8 ounces (225 g) **ground Italian sausage**
1 **large egg**
2 teaspoons **kosher salt**
1 tablespoon (6 g) freshly ground **black pepper**
2 teaspoons **garlic powder**
½ cup (120 ml) **bacon grease** (see page 148), divided
8 brioche buns or **Backyard Burger Buns** (page 34)
8 **slices Colby-Jack cheese**
8 **butter lettuce leaves**
¼ cup (60 g) **ketchup**

Serves 8

1. In a large mixing bowl, combine the ground beef, sausage, egg, salt, pepper, and garlic powder. Mix until uniformly combined. Form eight equal balls of the meat mixture.

2. Pour ¼ cup (60 ml) of bacon grease into a large cast-iron skillet and turn the heat to medium-high. Let the grease heat until it reaches 350°F (180°C). Carefully add the meat balls to the hot grease. You may need to work in batches, depending on how large your skillet is. With a heavy-duty spatula, press the balls as hard as you can to form super thin patties. The thinner the patty, the better the crust. Cook on the first side until a dark crust forms on the outer edges.

3. Now is the time to add more bacon grease— add a skosh to the uncooked sides of the burgers, then flip and cook the second side until your desired crust develops.

4. Some people like these burgers almost burnt/black. I like mine more dark brown, a steak-looking kind of sear.

5. Repeat, if necessary, until all the burgers are cooked.

6. To assemble, place the patties on the bottom buns. Top each with cheese and lettuce. Spread ketchup on the inside of each top bun and close the burgers.

STEAK FOR A CROWD

2 (6-pound, or 2.7 kg) **eye of round steaks**
½ cup (77 g) **Montreal steak seasoning**
¼ cup (40 g) **kosher salt**
¼ cup (24 g) freshly ground **black pepper**
¼ cup (36 g) **garlic powder**

Serves 20 to 30, often with some leftovers

If you ever need to make a lot of steak, for a lot of people, without a lot of money, I got you. I originally stumbled across this method when meal prepping. However, it eventually became my go-to on those nights I wanted a self-serve taco station for my teen's football team or a make-your-own steak sandwich setup for a group of friends. (Also great for stir-fries . . . you get the idea!) You can bake these instead of smoking, but of course with smoking you get the extra flavor and I find it easier to crank out those large batches in a short amount of time. You'll need wood or pellets of choice for smoking (I recommend hickory and/or mesquite for this recipe).

1. Lay one steak on an extra-large cutting board. Cut off any hard fat.

> **CHEAT CODE: Do not discard the trimmings. Once cooked down, this fat makes a tallow (see page 20), which can be used and stored just like oil, butter, or lard.**

2. Slice the meat into 1-inch (2.5 cm)-thick steaks. Transfer to a rimmed sheet pan or disposable 9 × 13-inch (23 × 33 cm) roasting pan while you prepare the rest of the meat. Repeat the process with the second steak, trimming away fat and slicing the beef into individual steaks.

3. Sprinkle the steak seasoning on both sides of the steaks.

4. Preheat the smoker (or grill) to 250°F (121°C).

5. When the smoker hits temperature, add the seasoned steaks. When organizing the steaks on the grill, the thicker steaks need to be closer to the heat source. Then, place the smaller steaks around them for more even cooking. Smoke the steaks until they reach an internal temperature of about 108°F (42°C), about 2 hours. Remove the steaks from the smoker.

6. Preheat the grill to 400°F (204°C).

7. Working in batches, if necessary, sear each steak for 1 to 2 minutes per side. This will help make a nice crust as well as cook the steaks to their final temperature. As far as temperature goes, when cooking for a big group that often includes kids, I like to aim for an internal temperature of 145°F (63°C), which for me ends up squarely in the medium-well camp after resting/carryover cooking. You can certainly go for another temp if you know your group prefers that. Let the steaks rest for a few minutes, then slice into strips and place them on a platter or in a chafing dish.

FAMILY NIGHT (OR GAME DAY) QUESADILLAS

This recipe includes three of my favorite things: steak, buttery carbs, and cheese. It's the perfect trifecta. When my kids were in the house, they'd ask me to make these at least twice a week. Thinking back, I can tell you why: Everyone got to build their own to their taste. One of my daughters, for example, always wanted straight meat and cheese, while another daughter wanted it fully loaded with veggies. I loved that you could easily customize these and crank them out in batches. And it was always a good time! Everyone would help and sit around the table while I cooked. They are super easy, but I do have one tip: It is imperative to get a hard, buttery crust on the outside of the quesadilla. Don't pull them off the heat too early!

SPICE RUBS

I love the Spiceology seasonings used here, but you can replace either pretty easily. The Cowboy Crust Espresso Chile Rub is a coffee-based rub with some chile. It gives you a darker sear and complex flavor. If you sub this one, make sure yours has both coffee and chile. The Pink Peppercorn Lemon Thyme can be replaced with a standard lemon pepper seasoning with a pinch of fresh lemon zest and dried herbs (thyme, of course, or try dried rosemary or parsley).

2 pounds (908 g) **skirt steak**

2 tablespoons (12 g) **Spiceology Cowboy Crust Espresso Chile Rub,** or preferred seasoning (see "Spice Rubs" below)

1 tablespoon **Spiceology Pink Peppercorn Lemon Thyme Blend** (see "Spice Rubs" below)

4 tablespoons (½ stick or 56 g) **butter,** divided

8 (8-inch, or 20 cm) **flour tortillas**

2 cups (225 g) shredded **cheddar cheese,** divided

½ cup (25 g) **sweet barbecue sauce** (like Sweet Baby Ray's), divided

Makes 4 quesadillas

1. We're going to start on our beef. Place the steak on a cutting board, sprinkle with the seasonings, and slice into ¼-inch (6 mm)-thick strips.

2. Heat a large cast-iron pan over medium-high heat. Add the steak and cook for 8 to 10 minutes, stirring often, until the meat is browned and cooked to your desired internal temperature. Set aside.

3. Heat a small, clean, well-seasoned cast-iron skillet or nonstick pan over medium heat.

> **CHEAT CODE: Definitely use a nonstick pan unless your cast iron is super well seasoned, or use Nonstick Cooking Spray (page 18, or store-bought) on the cast iron. You do not want stuck tortillas.**

4. Now, the quesadillas: Add 1 tablespoon (14 g) of butter to the pan to melt. Once the butter has melted, add 1 tortilla to the pan. Pile a quarter of the steak, 2 tablespoons of cheese (14 g), and 1 tablespoon (15.5 g) of barbecue sauce on the tortilla. Cover with another tortilla and let cook until the bottom tortilla is slightly browned and crispy, 1 to 2 minutes. Flip—carefully. Cook for 1 to 2 minutes more until golden brown and crispy on the bottom. Remove from the pan and serve. Repeat until you have made 4 quesadillas, adding butter before cooking each new batch.

PAN-FRIED STEAK + BETTER VEGGIES

Although you can serve any vegetable with this recipe, like cauliflower, bell peppers, broccoli, or asparagus, Brussels sprouts are near and dear to my heart. They were my number-one veg on my weight-loss journey and my signature veg when I launched my meal prep company. After cooking Brussels sprouts every which way for years, here's my biggest piece of advice: It's all about TLC while cooking. There's a fine line between perfect Brussels and overly charred.

4 (1-inch, or 2.5 cm)-thick **beef tenderloin steaks**

2 tablespoons (24 g) **SPG** (see page 17)

1 tablespoon (9.5 g) **Montreal steak seasoning** or your favorite steak seasoning

2 tablespoons (28 g) **butter**, divided

4 **garlic cloves**, crushed, divided

1 recipe **Better Brussels Sprouts** (page 150), or other vegetable of choice, prepared

Serves 4

1. Place the steaks on a large cutting board and season evenly with SPG and steak seasoning.

2. Heat a large cast-iron skillet over medium-high heat. Add 1 tablespoon (14 g) of butter to the skillet to melt. Add two steaks. Cook for 5 to 7 minutes until a blackened crust develops on the bottom. Add half the crushed garlic, flip the steaks, spoon butter and garlic from the skillet over the meat, and cook for 5 minutes more, or until the steaks reach your desired temperature (I like to cook mine to 135°F, or 57°C) and the crust is firm and crispy. Remove the steaks from the skillet and let rest on a cutting board. Repeat with the remaining steaks, butter, and garlic.

3. Serve with Better Brussels Sprouts or veggie of your choice.

A5 + EGG

2 teaspoons **dried rosemary**

2 teaspoons **dried minced garlic**

2 (4- to 5-ounce, or 115 to 140 g) **A5 Wagyu Zabuton** or **Denver steaks**

½ teaspoon **flaky salt**

¼ teaspoon freshly ground **black pepper**

1½ teaspoons **butter**

2 **large eggs**

Serves 2

When I moved to Texas, the access to cattle is something I never experienced before in my life. I now know so many of my local butchers and so, of course, sometimes I splurge on a special treat. Now, let me just say, this is my treat dinner for the wife and me. We rarely get to eat like this—and when you do, go for it. Take the extra effort to make an herb packet, keeping the butter cleaner and removing any potential bitterness from the rosemary stem.

The A5 Wagyu Zabuton is known for its marbling and tenderness. But maybe you want a somewhat fancy and not super-extravagant night. In that case, ask the butcher for a "Denver steak" and it's fine if it's not an A5. While the other steak recipes in this book use common cuts, this is a less common cut that I wanted to highlight. See, the Denver steak is cut from the under blade portion of the chuck roll. The beef chuck is the shoulder, which obviously gets a lot of movement. But the one part that doesn't is the portion under the blade. Here's the thought process: The steaks cut from the parts that move a lot, like eye of round, are tough. The parts that don't move are extremely tender. The Denver is the one part of the shoulder that doesn't get a lot of movement, so it's a juicy cut of beef.

Okay, last but not least by much, if you see a rib eye with incredible marbling, plug it into this recipe. The late addition of black pepper and the herb sachet will help it shine. And note, you will need cheesecloth and butcher twine for this recipe.

1. First, let's use a little hack to infuse herb flavor in your steaks. Lay out a small piece of cheesecloth and place the rosemary and garlic in the center. Pull up the sides of the cheesecloth and secure the bundle with butcher twine. Set aside.

2. Heat a large cast-iron skillet over high heat (like 400°F, or 204°C, minimum). Sprinkle each steak with ¼ teaspoon of salt (do not add the pepper yet, as pepper can turn bitter at high heat and will affect the flavor of the steak—important when you are cooking high-end steaks). Place the steaks in the hot skillet and sear each side until you get a good crust—probably 30 to 45 seconds. Season with the pepper.

3. Add the butter and herb packet to the skillet. Using tongs, constantly stir the herb packet in the butter until the butter melts and begins to brown. Move the herb packet to one side of the skillet. Continuously spoon the browned butter over the steaks for 1 to 2 minutes, flip, and cook an additional 1 to 2 minutes until the meat has reached your desired temperature. When I'm making steak and eggs, I cook my steak to medium-rare (130°F, or 54°C). Transfer to a plate but leave the heat on. Let the steaks rest for 5 minutes while you prepare your eggs.

4. Crack the eggs into the skillet. Cook for 1 to 2 minutes per side until the whites are set and the yolks are runny—or to your preferred style and doneness. Serve the eggs with the steaks.

PROPER PULLED PORK

+

EASY VINEGAR SLAW

When it comes to smoking, it's true there are some recipes that take years to master and there are all sorts of insider secrets. (Yes, I'm thinking of brisket. That is not an easy day of smoking.) Then, over on the other side, we've got pork shoulder. Yes, it takes 8 to 10 hours to cook low and slow, but the cut is forgiving. I overcooked one by accident and it was still juicy and tasted great. My recipe here is meant for entry-level smokers and anyone who just wants an easy all-day cook with a big, satisfying reward.

Okay, a word on pork rubs. My current favorite is Spiceology's Smoky Honey Habanero. But I mix it up all the time. The amount of rub you'll use in this recipe is not going to take over. Feel free to buy a different pork rub (sometimes called "butt rub") or use your favorite jar if you have a house recipe. You'll need wood or pellets of choice for smoking (I use cherry and hickory for this recipe).

FOR THE PULLED PORK

1 (4-pound, or 1.8 kg) **bone-in pork shoulder**
¼ cup (weight varies) **pork seasoning blend**
½ cup (120 ml) **rye whiskey**

FOR SERVING

8 **sesame brioche buns**
1 cup (250 g) **barbecue sauce**
1½ cups (330 g) **Easy Vinegar Slaw** (page 52) or store-bought
¼ cup (40 g) **Quick-Pickled Onions** (page 48)
½ cup (78 g) **pickle slices**

Serves 8

1. To make the pulled pork, pat your pork dry using a paper towel. Then, with a knife, score the fat cap to expose more of the meat. This will create crunchy ends. Gently pat the pork seasoning evenly on all sides of the meat. Use your fingers to push some of the seasoning into the openings you made when scoring the meat.

2. Preheat the smoker to 250°F (121°C) and add cherry and hickory wood to your wood box.

3. Place the pork on the grill grate. If your smoker does not have a drip tray, place a disposable aluminum 9 × 13-inch (23 × 33 cm) roasting pan on the bottom rack of your smoker, directly underneath the pork shoulder. Let cook until the pork reaches an internal temperature of 165°F (74°C), about 5 to 6 hours, depending on the size of the meat.

4. Line a large disposable roasting pan with butcher paper and transfer the pork to the pan.

5. Remove the drip pan with the drippings. Stir the rye whiskey into the drippings and pour the mixture over the pork. Fold the butcher paper over the meat and cover the pan with aluminum foil. Return the pork to the smoker and cook until it reaches an internal temperature of about 203°F (95°C), about 1 to 2 hours.

The entire cook time for this pork is long. It may take up to 10 hours to reach the final temperature. Be patient. It will get there.

Continued on next page...

6. Remove the pork from the smoker and let it rest, covered, for 30 minutes to 1 hour. Uncover the meat and transfer it to a clean pan. Using two large forks, or the pork bone, shred the meat. Pour any remaining drippings over the shredded meat.

CHEAT CODE: At this point, you can add more rub, to taste, to the drippings if you want to punch up the flavor.

7. Now, assemble. Slather barbecue sauce on the bottom half of each bun, add 2 or 3 tablespoons (27 to 40.5 g) of slaw, pile on a generous helping of pulled pork, and finish with pickled onions and pickle slices as you like. Add the top bun to close the sandwich. You're ready to serve.

Keep an eye out for deals. When choosing a cut of meat, keep in mind that a Boston butt has more intermuscular fat than a pork picnic shoulder, which is the leaner of the two cuts.

EASY VINEGAR SLAW

One of my local stores makes an absolutely killer vinegar-based slaw. But I realize I am in Texas and my access to delicious BBQ and sides is better than most. If you need to make your own to complete this sandwich, I got you.

½ of a **small head of green cabbage**, finely shredded
1 **carrot**, peeled and finely shredded
⅛ cup thinly sliced **red onion** (optional)
¼ cup **apple cider vinegar**
⅛ cup **neutral oil**
½ tablespoon **sugar**
½ tablespoon **Dijon mustard**
¼ teaspoon **kosher salt**
¼ teaspoon **freshly ground black pepper**

1. Combine all the vegetables in a large mixing bowl. In a small mixing bowl, whisk the remaining ingredients. Taste and adjust to your liking (some people might like more sugar or mustard). You can salt to taste now as well, but I usually wait until it's tossed with the veg to get a better read on it.

2. Add about two-thirds of the dressing to the vegetables and stir. If you want to add more dressing at this point, feel free. But remember, the cabbage will release some moisture as well, so don't go too wet. Add more salt and pepper if needed.

Yields 5–6 cups, enough for the sandwiches and to use as a side if you want.

QUICK-PICKLED ONIONS

Unlike traditional pickles, these don't take a long amount of time. While they get better as the week goes on, they are ready to use as little as an hour after you make them.

1 **red onion**
3 or 4 **garlic cloves**, peeled
½ cup (120 ml) **white vinegar**
½ cup (120 ml) **red wine vinegar**
1½ cups (360 ml) **water**
¼ cup (50 g) **sugar**
1 teaspoon **kosher salt**
1 teaspoon freshly ground **black pepper**

Makes about 1 cup (105 g)

1. Thinly slice the red onion and crush the garlic with the side of a knife. Transfer both to a pint-size (480 ml) Mason jar or similar container.

2. In a medium-size saucepan over medium-high heat, heat the white and red wine vinegars, water, sugar, and salt until the sugar and salt are dissolved. Remove from the heat and carefully pour the mixture into the jar with the onion and garlic and let cool at room temperature for 1 hour. Seal the jar and refrigerate until ready to use, or up to 1 week.

See photo on next page.

Quick-Pickled Onions, page 51

THE BOILED BURGER

As a content creator, I have come across a LOT of crazy viral trends. However the boiled burger is one of the few that I've tested—and it just works. Boiling it gives you a ton of juiciness and removes some natural sodium from the meat. As a fan of sous vide burgers (see Super Sous Vide Burgers, page 32), I was curious. So, I tried the boiling method and was a little shocked to find out you could, indeed, get a nice crust on a boiled burger. While I prefer traditional grilled burgers or sous vide, in most cases, these burgers are great when you're hosting an event. The boiled burgers stay juicy, and you can just sear them to order when people are ready to eat.

FOR THE BURGERS

1 cup (240 ml) **bone broth**
¾ cup (180 ml) **water**
1 pound (454 g) **lean ground beef**
1 tablespoon (18 g) **Better Than Bouillon Sautéed Onion Base**
1 teaspoon **kosher salt**
1 teaspoon freshly ground **black pepper**
1 teaspoon **garlic powder**

FOR SERVING

4 **burger buns** (ideally brioche)
4 **slices cheddar cheese**
4 **butter lettuce leaves**
½ **red onion**, thinly sliced
4 tablespoons (60 g) **mayonnaise**

Serves 4

1. To make the burgers, in a large skillet with deep sides over high heat, bring the bone broth and water to a boil. Reduce the heat to medium-high to keep the liquid at a simmer.

2. Meanwhile, in a large bowl, mix the ground beef, onion base, salt, pepper, and garlic powder. Form four equal patties from the meat mixture, then place them in the skillet. Cover and simmer for 15 to 20 minutes until the meat reaches an internal temperature of about 145°F (63°C).

If you prefer a more well-done burger, you can certainly cook it to a higher internal temperature.

3. Heat a cast-iron skillet over medium-high heat. Sear off the patties in the skillet, about 1 minute per side, working in batches if necessary so as not to crowd the pan.

4. To serve the burgers, place a patty on the bottom half of a bun. Top with a slice of cheese, a lettuce leaf, and onion slices. Spread 1 tablespoon (15 g) of mayonnaise on the top half of a bun and close the burger.

CHEAT CODE: To elevate this dish, see Super Sous Vide Burgers (page 32) for putting a crust on the burger bun.

TEXAS BRISKET WITH A TWIST (OR TWO)

1 (12- to 14-pound, or 5.5 to 6.3 kg) **whole brisket**
1 to 2 cups (weight varies) **seasoning blend of choice**

Serves 8 to 12

Make sure your brisket is completely covered in seasoning. I do either classic, SPG, or sweet, which has brown sugar in it. Keep in mind, the brown sugar will caramelize a skosh and help your crust along.

I have cooked a lot of brisket for my family as it wasn't always such a sought-after (read expensive) cut of meat. And, while the cost has gone up, we still love it. A classic Texas brisket is smoked between 250°F and 275°F (121°C and 135°C). I do mine at 225°F (107°C). I only do this on a larger whole packer, which is 10 pounds (4.5 kg) or more, but I feel as though it allows the intramuscular fat to render better than smoking hotter. To me, it's a more reliably juicy brisket . . . but it is, admittedly, my twist on a classic.

Typically, Texas-style brisket is wrapped in aluminum foil, so you spend 8 to 9 hours getting crust and then you steam it in the foil. I have an issue with that. So, my other twist is swapping in butcher paper, which is breathable, allowing some steaming but also allowing moisture in and out to keep the integrity of the bark.

Okay, there are my twists. Ready for tips? I try to trim and season the brisket the night before. Okay, stick with me one more minute as we talk binders. I am "Team No Binder." I have done side by side with mustard and without mustard. The whole purpose of the mustard binder is to give you a layer of moisture to help the rub adhere to the meat. But if you trim and season and let the meat sweat in the fridge overnight, the meat creates its own natural binder. Then, the next day, just take the brisket out early so it can come up to room temperature before smoking. Speaking of smoking, I recommend post oak wood or pellets for this recipe.

1. Using a knife and large cutting board, make the brisket uniform by removing all the silver skin, excess fat, and uneven portions. (Don't toss the trimmings! Make tallow, see page 20.)

> **CHEAT CODE: If you get home and open a full brisket to discover a huge piece of fat in the middle, feel free to cut it out while trimming your brisket before seasoning. If it does not have that huge piece of fat, you can trim without touching it and trim out the interior fat when slicing your brisket.**

2. Next, season the meat with about half of the seasoning mix. Never rub your seasoning in—pat it in. As you're patting in the seasoning, take note of which way the grain is running so when the brisket is ready to serve, you can create tender slices by cutting against, or across, the grain. Cover the brisket and let it rest in the fridge for 2 hours, or ideally, overnight.

Continued on next page...

THE BEND TEST

When I'm in the store picking out a brisket, I always do the bend test. Grab a brisket by the ends and pull the ends inward toward each other. A brisket with less fat will have more bend. Since this fat will not render down and is usually removed, selecting a brisket that has more bend than others will mean less prep work for you.

3. Remove the brisket from the fridge, place it on a large cutting board on the counter, and let it rest for an hour at room temperature.

4. Add another layer of seasoning with the remaining rub mix.

5. Preheat the smoker or grill to 225°F (107°C).

6. Place a disposable aluminum roasting pan on the bottom rack of the smoker or grill to catch any drippings from the brisket. Place your wood chips in a piece of aluminum foil. Fold the foil over the chips and set them on the bottom rack off to the side of your drippings pan. Transfer the brisket to the top rack of the smoker, fat-side down. Cook to an internal temperature of 202°F to 203°F (94°C to 95°C), about 6 hours.

7. While the brisket cooks, prepare a cooler for a "hot hold" by lining the bottom of the cooler with a towel. Remove the brisket from the smoker and place it on a piece of butcher's paper. Tightly wrap the meat with the paper and fold the sides in to close the package. Place the brisket in the cooler with the lid closed for 1 to 2 hours. A hot hold allows the brisket the critical time it needs to rest before serving.

8. When you're ready to serve the brisket, remove it from the cooler, uncover, and slice across the grain, creating ¼-inch (6 mm)-thick slices. Slicing against the grain is critical when slicing brisket. If you slice it with the grain, the brisket will be tough and chewy—it can ruin the brisket. Against the grain will yield a tender, melt-in-your-mouth bite.

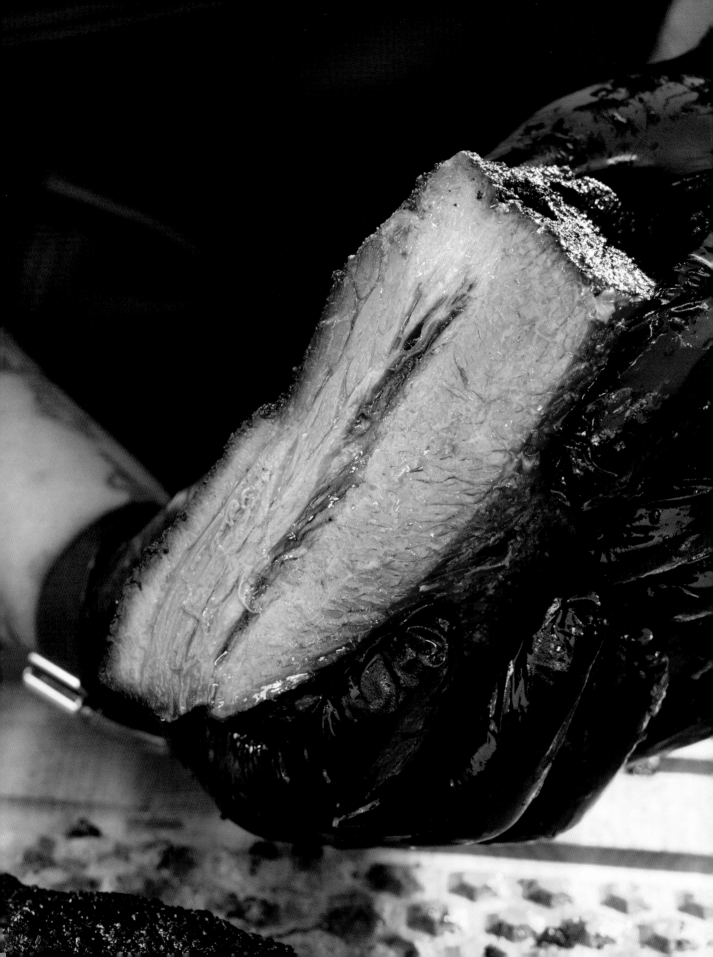

DINO RIBS

1 (3-bone) **plate rib**

1 cup (192 g) **SPG** (see page 17)
When I make ribs, I like to really cover the surface with rub.

Serves 4

Okay, so a hill I'm willing to die on is that beef ribs are the best bite in barbecue. Yes, better than brisket. However, my favorite beef rib, the plate rib (a.k.a. the dino rib), is expensive and can be hard to find. However, its little brother, the beef rib, is easy to find—and it's not sought after, so you may even find it on sale. Just don't spread the word. If you do things right, you can get a similar bite to a plate rib out of this humbler cut. So, by all means, go for the dino rib here, if you can get it. If not, check out page 60 for my back rib take on it. You also need wood or pellets of choice for smoking.

1. Start by trimming the hard fat on the fat cap side of the slab. Place the trimmed meat on a baking sheet. I enjoy these ribs with and without the membrane, so do whatever you'd like. Cover the ribs in SPG.

2. Preheat the smoker or grill to 250°F (121°C).

3. Place the ribs on the top rack of the smoker, or wherever gives you the most consistent probe reading at 250°F (121°C). Close the grill lid and cook for 2 hours to an internal temperature between 165°F and 170°F (74°C and 77°C).

4. Remove the ribs from the smoker and set the smoker temperature to 325°F (163°C) so it can rise in temperature while you work. Place the ribs on a sheet of butcher paper or heavy-duty aluminum foil and wrap them in the paper. Return the ribs to the grill and cook until they reach 202°F to 203°F (94°C to 95°C), about 1 to 2 hours. Remove the ribs from the smoker and let rest for 2 hours, wrapped. Then unwrap, slice, and serve.

POOR MAN'S DINO RIBS

Beef back ribs are generally leaner than plate short ribs or chuck short ribs, but with a little bit of TLC they can be juicy and tender.

1 rack **beef back ribs** (about 2 pounds, or 908 g)

1 cup (192 g) **SPG** (see page 17)

When I make ribs, I like to really cover the surface with rub.

1/3 cup (80 ml) freshly squeezed **orange juice**

2 tablespoons (30 ml) **vinegar** (white, red wine, or apple cider)

Serves 4

1. Start by trimming your meat on a large cutting board. Use a sharp knife to remove any excess or hard fat and silver skin. Place the trimmed ribs on a baking sheet. Sprinkle SPG on both sides of the meat, cover with plastic wrap, then refrigerate for 1 hour.

2. While the meat rests, make the baste. In a small bowl, stir together the orange juice and vinegar. It should taste like an unseasoned vinaigrette—sweet with just a little bit of a kick to it.

3. Preheat the smoker or grill to 250°F (121°C).

4. Remove the plastic wrap from the ribs and spoon half of the orange juice and vinegar mixture onto the meat. Place the meat in the smoker or on the grill over indirect heat. Close the smoker lid and cook for 2 hours. Open the lid and spoon the remaining orange juice mixture on the meat. Close the lid and cook for an additional 1 to 2 hours until the internal temperature reaches about 170° (77°C). Remove the ribs from the smoker and let rest for 1 hour, wrapped. Then unwrap, slice, and serve.

THREE-FOR-ONE SPARERIBS

2 racks **pork ribs** (4 to 5 pounds, or 1.8 to 2.3 kg, total)

3 tablespoons (36 g) **SPG** (see page 17)

¾ cup (or more; weight varies) preferred **rib rub**

When I make these ribs, the flesh side is completely covered in seasoning and I highly recommend it. I use all sorts of rubs, too, from classic pork rubs to cherry chipotle to honey garlic. I love getting some sweetness in there with the savory. If your rub is not sweet, add a ¼ cup (60 g) packed brown sugar.

Serves 4

Okay, soapbox moment: I want to talk about buying the full sparerib vs. the precut. Buying the full rib gives you three different bites as it relates to ribs. With a full sparerib, you get the squared-off rib, the rib tip, and the flat meat you can cook as well. The rib tip is going to have a juicier, fattier bite, so if you have somebody who likes that kind of rib, the addition of the rib tips to the party will make them very happy. Depending on whom you talk to, there are different opinions on silver skin. I like to trim mine but, if you choose to leave on, get a hard char on the side with the silver skin. It's like an attached pork chip. Use wood or pellets of choice for smoking.

1. Pat your ribs with a paper towel. Place them on a large cutting board. Cut through the cartilage along the end of the longest bone to separate the rib tips from the ribs. Skirt meat, found on the back side of the ribs near the middle, will cook unevenly and should be removed. Now, remove the silver skin. Any loose flaps or pieces are going to overcook, so slice those off as well. You can also slice off the ends of the meat to create nice square edges to promote even cooking, if you'd like.

2. Next, pat your SPG and rib rub onto the meat. Make sure to get good coverage.

3. Reheat the smoker or grill to 250°F (121°C).

4. Place the ribs in the smoker and let them ride for about 2½ hours. After that, remove them from the grill, wrap them tightly in butcher paper or heavy-duty aluminum foil, return the ribs to the grill, and crank up the heat to 350°F (180°C). Let cook until you reach your desired doneness. If you're going for fall-off-the-bone tender, you want to cook to an internal temperature of between 202°F and 203°F (94°C and 95°C).

CHEAT CODE: If your ribs are done but your guests haven't arrived yet, do a hot hold. Line the bottom of the cooler with a towel, then place the ribs (still wrapped in butcher paper or foil) in the cooler and close the lid. This will keep the ribs ready to eat for up to 7 hours if you have a quality cooler. (Why 7 hours? Well, I won a bet with a friend that it would work that long!)

RIB TIPS

An advantage to using a dry rub is that you're not adding a moisture source, like butter or beef stock, to the meat, so you maintain the bark while the meat is wrapped.

I have had better results double-wrapping versus single-wrapping my ribs.

3

Healthy-ish Dinners

As you might guess if you know anything about how much I love food, I don't eat healthy every night. But I try to keep healthy-ish dinners in rotation every week for sure. Now some, like the Designated Hitter Grilled Chicken or Jumbo Shrimp and Veggies, are actually objectively healthy. Others are meant more to keep me from eating something truly unhealthy—think air fryer wings or crispy catfish. The cheat code here is taking a clean piece of meat and adding razzle-dazzle to make your taste buds happy without full-on deep-frying.

SECRET BRINE SKILLET CHICKEN

4 **boneless, skinless chicken breasts**

4 cups (960 ml) **pickle juice**

3 tablespoons (45 ml) **olive oil**, divided, plus
more as needed

2 (12-ounce, or 340 g) packages **pre-riced
cauliflower**

*Note: Many grocery stores now sell this in the produce section.
I recommend that over frozen.*

2 **green bell peppers**

1 **red onion**, sliced

2½ teaspoons **kosher salt**, divided

1 tablespoon (7 g) **smoked paprika**

Serves 4

Chicken is one of the most popular things to make for dinner, so it's no surprise that when I had a meal prep company, chicken was in demand. But reheating chicken is tough. It's so easy to dry it out. The thing I had to figure out was how to make the chicken taste good not only when it's first cooked but also when reheated. The answer was not in the cooking but in brining. It lets the chicken hold more moisture, making it super juicy initially and not a bit dry when reheated.

Now, let's talk pickle brine. Candidly, I think when you go with a longer brine (anywhere from overnight to twenty-four hours), the chicken usually ends up a little too pickle-y. My recommendation? Go somewhere between two and four hours. If the inside of the chicken is pink, but the outside has a green tint, you've nailed it. I'll be honest, I never taste pickle in this dish. Although there is more flavor than a saltwater brine, it's subtle.

1. First, you're going to soak your chicken breast in pickle brine. Place the breasts in an extra-large zip-top plastic bag and pour the pickle juice in the bag. Seal the bag and place it in the fridge for 2 to 4 hours.

> **CHEAT CODE: Follow the directions! Do not let this brine overnight. I hear you—sometimes I let my marinades or brines sit overnight. But if you do it with this recipe, it will not turn out right.**

2. Heat a large skillet over medium-high heat. Add 1 tablespoon (15 ml) of olive oil and swirl to coat the skillet. Add your riced cauliflower and cook for 5 to 7 minutes until slightly browned and warm. Divide the cauliflower rice among four plates.

3. While your cauliflower cooks, cut the green bell peppers into ½-inch (1 cm)-thick slices. After you remove the cauliflower from the skillet, return the skillet to the heat and add 1 tablespoon (15 ml) of olive oil. Add the onion, bell peppers, and ½ teaspoon of salt and cook for 4 to 5 minutes until slightly tender. Divide the vegetables among the plates.

4. Remove the chicken from the brine and pat dry with a paper towel. Slice the breasts lengthwise to make two thin pieces of chicken per breast. Sprinkle evenly with the remaining 2 teaspoons of salt and the smoked paprika over both sides of each piece of chicken.

5. Heat another large skillet over medium-high heat and add the remaining 1 tablespoon (15 ml) of olive oil to the skillet. Add the chicken to the hot pan and cook for 4 to 5 minutes per side until cooked through (the internal temperature should reach 165°F [74°C]) and browned. You may need to work in batches, adding additional oil to the pan as needed. Transfer the chicken to a cutting board and let rest for 5 to 10 minutes. Cut it into thick strips and add to the plates.

GO-TO GRILLED CHICKEN

1 tablespoon (6 g) freshly ground **black pepper**
2 teaspoons **kosher salt**
2 teaspoons **paprika**
2 teaspoons **onion powder**
1 teaspoon **garlic powder**
4 **boneless, skinless chicken breasts**
2 tablespoons (30 ml) **extra-virgin olive oil**

Serves 4

1. Preheat the grill to 400°F (204°C).

2. In a small bowl, stir together the pepper, salt, paprika, onion powder, and garlic powder. Brush the chicken with olive oil, then sprinkle the seasoning evenly over both sides of the chicken. Transfer the chicken to the grill and cook over direct heat for 7 to 8 minutes per side, or until the internal temperature reaches 165°F (74°C). When you slice into your chicken, the juices should be clear. Let rest for 5 minutes and serve.

Looking for clean char marks on your meat? Don't flip it too early. Let it cook a full 6 minutes or so before taking a gentle peek underneath to make sure char marks have formed—then you can flip. Never flip back and forth multiple times as you cook. Not only does this ruin the potential of clean char marks, but it also makes it harder to gauge when the chicken is done since both sides will appear cooked before the middle of the breast is done cooking.

Want square char marks? Simply rotate the meat 90 degrees after 3 to 4 minutes, then, when you flip it and work on the next side, do the same thing.

THE WEEKNIGHT STIR-FRY

1 cup (200 g) **extra-long-grain white rice**
2 tablespoons (30 ml) **sesame oil**, divided
1 pound (454 g) **ground turkey**
1 **red bell pepper**, thinly sliced
1 **orange bell pepper**, thinly sliced
1 **zucchini**, diced
½ **red onion**, cut into ¼-inch (6 mm)-thick slices
¼ teaspoon **kosher salt**
¼ teaspoon freshly ground **black pepper**
Handful **fresh basil leaves**
¼ teaspoon **sesame seeds**
Spicy mayonnaise (see Veggie Sandwiches, page 136) or store-bought, for serving

Whenever there's ground turkey involved in a recipe, it's a callback to weight loss for me. At first, when I started eating ground turkey, I wasn't a fan. Then, I learned a lot by cooking it over the course of a few years (yes, years). Eventually, I came around to it. I learned turkey is generally going to be drier than ground beef because there's less fat, but proper seasoning can solve some of that. But, ultimately, my answer is to use it in recipes where it can absorb some moisture and you don't miss that extra helping of fat, like this stir-fry. With lots of vegetables, including zucchini, you'll get plenty of moisture. And, in my opinion, this is just so fresh with sesame oil, sesame seeds, and fresh basil that I don't feel the need to add a seasoning blend. I do, though, love a hit of spicy mayo on the plate.

Serves 4

1. Begin by cooking the rice according to the package instructions (see sidebar below).

2. Heat a large nonstick skillet over medium-high heat. Add 1 tablespoon (15 ml) of sesame oil to the skillet and swirl to coat. Add the ground turkey to the pan and cook for 7 to 8 minutes, stirring to break up the meat, until browned and cooked through. Remove from the skillet.

3. Return the skillet to the stovetop and increase the heat to high. Add the remaining 1 tablespoon (15 ml) of sesame oil to the pan. Add the bell peppers, zucchini, and onion and sauté for 4 to 5 minutes until the vegetables are charred on the outside but still tender on the inside. Return the turkey to the pan and season with the pepper. Stir together and cook for 1 to 2 minutes more.

4. To serve, split the rice and stir-fry evenly among four plates. (To plate as pictured, use a mold to shape the rice.) Garnish generously with fresh basil and sesame seeds and add a dollop of spicy mayo to each plate.

BRING IN THE BROTH

When cooking rice, I often like to swap some of the water for broth. It's a little trick to get more flavor and also a few more nutrients. In this recipe, I recommend swapping ½ cup (120 ml) of chicken broth for ½ cup (120 ml) of water. If the directions say to use 2 cups (480 ml) of water for 1 cup (200 g) of rice, swap out ½ cup (120 ml) for broth.

THE WEEKEND STIR-FRY

½ cup (120 g) packed **brown sugar**

¼ cup (60 ml) **soy sauce**

2 tablespoons (40 g) **maple syrup**

1 tablespoon (15 ml) **apple cider vinegar**

1 teaspoon **Dijon mustard**

½ teaspoon **smoked paprika**

¼ teaspoon freshly ground **black pepper**

2 tablespoons (30 ml) **avocado oil**

1 pound (454 g) **boneless, skinless chicken breast**, thinly sliced

1 cup (100 g) **green beans**

1 cup (120 g) quartered **zucchini**

1 cup (75 g) thinly sliced **carrot**

1 **shallot**, thinly sliced

2 **garlic cloves**, minced

1 tablespoon (6 g) **scallions** (green part only), thinly sliced on the diagonal

Serves 4

If the Weeknight Stir-Fry (page 72) is a little too "healthy-ish" for you, this recipe is the move. With the "dry" style of stir-fry in the weeknight version, you don't add as much sodium or calories. This version still has a healthy protein, but you've got more sugar by far and a bit more sodium . . . and, of course, more calories. But it's closer to a hibachi-type stir-fry, and when you're cooking for the whole family, this is easier to sell to the kids. The flavor is on the sweet side with brown sugar and maple syrup, but balanced with the vinegar and Dijon mustard. Oh, and swap out the vinegar for white or red wine vinegar for flavor variations.

1. In a medium-size bowl, whisk the brown sugar, soy sauce, maple syrup, vinegar, mustard, paprika, and pepper until combined. Set aside.

2. Heat a wok or large skillet over medium-high heat. Add the avocado oil and swirl to coat the skillet. Add the chicken and cook until browned but not cooked through, 2 to 3 minutes per side. Add all the veggies— the green beans, zucchini, carrot, shallot, and garlic. Cook for 4 to 5 minutes until the veg are tender and the chicken has reached an internal temperature of 165°F (74°C).

3. Stir in the soy sauce mixture and bring to a boil. Remove from the heat and transfer to plates. Garnish with scallions to serve.

JUMBO SHRIMP + VEGGIES

Growing up, I most often remember eating shrimp cooked in butter. Cooking shrimp that way adds extra calories and fat, but worse, it can make them on the soggy side. Grilling big, juicy shrimp, on the other hand, will give you more of a steak-like texture. Unlike salmon, which I actually don't prefer cooking on the grill, the shrimp keep enough of their moisture so you get the grilled flavor on the outside while staying succulent on the inside.

In this recipe, I keep the shrimp simple. If you have fresh, large shrimp, you don't want them hiding behind a seasoning blend. But the veggies, on the other hand, I love really going for it with the seasoning before I grill them. There's nothing wrong with simply grilled veg, either, but I think the more assertive vegetables here are a better counterpoint to the shrimp. (Note: These also make great taco fillings.)

SMALL BUT TASTY

Have shrimpy shrimp? This recipe works with just about any shrimp, but the smaller the shrimp, the shorter the cook time.

FOR THE VEGGIES

1 tablespoon (15 ml) **avocado oil**
¼ teaspoon **kosher salt**
¼ teaspoon freshly ground **black pepper**
¼ teaspoon **paprika**
¼ teaspoon **cayenne pepper**
¼ teaspoon **red pepper flakes**
¼ teaspoon **dried oregano**
¼ teaspoon **ground cumin**
1 **red bell pepper**, halved
1 **orange bell pepper**, halved
1 **head broccoli**

FOR THE SHRIMP

16 (about 1½ pounds, or 681 g) **large, raw jumbo shrimp**, peeled and deveined
½ teaspoon freshly squeezed **lime juice**
Avocado oil cooking spray
½ teaspoon **SPG** (see page 17)

Serves 4

1. Preheat the grill to medium-high heat (350°F to 400°F, or 180°C to 204°C).

2. To make the veggies, in a large bowl, whisk the avocado oil, salt, pepper, paprika, cayenne, red pepper flakes, oregano, and cumin to blend. Toss the bell pepper halves in the oil mixture. To get an even coating, shake them around. Transfer the peppers to the grill, placing directly on the grill grates over direct heat. Reserve the bowl. Cook for 10 to 15 minutes until the outside is charred and the veggies are between tender and crisp (I call this the veggie version of al dente). Transfer to a cutting board.

3. While the peppers cook, repeat the process with the broccoli, tossing it in the remaining oil, coating evenly, then adding it directly to the grill over direct heat. The broccoli will take 20 to 25 minutes to cook through. Flip it every 5 to 10 minutes. Transfer the broccoli to the cutting board with the peppers and let cool for 5 minutes. Thinly slice the peppers, then, on a large cutting board, use a knife to remove the broccoli florets from the stalk and chop into bite-size pieces.

4. Thread 4 shrimp onto each of 4 wooden skewers. Brush with the lime juice, spritz with cooking spray, and sprinkle with SPG. Grill over direct heat for 2 to 3 minutes per side until the shrimp are bright pink. The internal temperature should read 145°F (63°C). Serve with the veggies for jumbo flavor.

HERB-CRUSTED SALMON

You know what's funny about this recipe is that you might see me using Dijon mustard instead of egg wash and think that was my secret ingredient. You're partially right. The mustard coat is almost undetectable, but vinegar is in most mustards and works wonders on proteins from salmon to pork, whatever. It helps the seasoning adhere to the flesh but also delivers a more tender flake when you bite into the salmon. And it helps you build a thicker crust, undoubtedly.

But the mustard also gets some help. The star here is the cheese. A blend of two cheeses turns the crust from an herb-y panko standard to something that's almost as addictively crunchy as one of those tacos that uses cheese as the taco shell. This is fast-food level crave-ability and crunch meets salmon.

1½ cups (150 g) **panko** (Japanese) **bread crumbs**
3 tablespoons (12 g) **fresh parsley**, chopped
1 tablespoon (4 g) **fresh dill**
1 tablespoon (2 g) **fresh thyme leaves**
1 teaspoon **lemon zest**
1 teaspoon **lime zest**
½ cup (60 g) dry grated **parmesan cheese** (from a shaker!)
1 cup (115 g) shredded **mozzarella cheese**
3 tablespoons (45 g) **Dijon mustard**
4 (6-ounce, or 170 g) **salmon fillets**
1 tablespoon (12 g) **SPG** (see page 17)

Serves 4

1. Preheat the oven to 400°F (204°C). Line a rimmed sheet pan with parchment paper.

2. In a large bowl, combine the bread crumbs, parsley, dill, thyme, lemon zest, and lime zest. Stir well to combine, then add the cheeses and stir to make sure they are evenly distributed.

3. Brush mustard on both sides of the salmon fillets. Sprinkle the SPG evenly across the fillets, taking care to season each side of each piece of salmon. Dip each fillet in the panko mixture, coating all sides evenly. Place the salmon on the prepared sheet pan.

4. Bake for 12 to 17 minutes until the salmon is flaky, or until the internal temperature reaches 145°F (63°C).

LEMONY SALMON BELLY WITH A SAFFRON KICKER

FOR THE BRINE

1 **lemon**

FOR THE SALMON

4 (6-ounce, or 170 g) **skin-on salmon fillets**
1 tablespoon (14 g) **salted butter**
1 tablespoon (10 g) minced **garlic**
1 teaspoon freshly ground **black pepper**

FOR THE RICE

1 cup (200 g) **extra-long-grain white rice**
Pinch **saffron threads**, plus a few more threads
    for garnish

Serves 4

I feel like the salmon belly is the best part of the fillet, and the skin is underrated when you fry it hard and get a chip-like consistency. This is hard to do with the loin as you might overcook the flesh, but because the belly is thicker, you can sear the skin side hot and fast and not overcook the meat. Also, you'll find it has a thin layer of fat between the skin and flesh so the fat-to-meat ratio on a belly reminds me of a top-quality steak, like an A5. The acidity from the lemon helps break down the proteins. Combined with the chip-like skin, it's the perfect bite.

I often see saffron in very complex recipes. As expensive as it is, I love using it to speak on its own. White rice, being basic and bland in nature so to speak, is the perfect canvas. To plate this dish, think of the salmon belly as a loaded cracker. The skin is so crunchy it will literally crack.

1. Start with the brine. Zest the whole lemon in a gallon-size resealable plastic bag, then cut the lemon in half and squeeze the juice of ½ lemon into the bag as well.

2. To make the salmon, add the fillets to the bag, seal the bag, and refrigerate overnight.

3. The next day, to make the rice, begin by cooking it according to the package instructions (see sidebar, page 72), adding the saffron with the water.

4. While the rice cooks, work on the salmon. Heat a large skillet over medium-high heat. Add the butter and garlic. Once the butter melts and the garlic becomes fragrant, place the salmon, skin-side down, in the skillet. Cook for 4 to 5 minutes, basting the fish with the butter and juices in the skillet, which will create a nice crust. Turn the heat down to medium, flip the salmon over to the flesh side, sprinkle with pepper, and cook for 4 to 5 minutes more, basting continuously while cooking, until flaky and the internal temperature reaches 145°F (63 °C).

When flipping the salmon, you can check whether the skin is done by scraping the skin gently with a knife. It should make a noise like you're scraping a knife across toast.

5. Transfer the salmon belly to a cutting board and cut it into bite-size pieces. Divide the salmon among four plates. Stack a skosh of rice on each piece of salmon. Place a few saffron threads on top and serve.

6. Saffron is one of the most expensive spices out there. However, when you add it to a basic dish, like white rice, it really makes an impact. People buy saffron and mix it in with a thousand other spices, but when you let it breathe on its own, it really shows its flavor profile. Even if you haven't had saffron before, it's a great way to set your palate.

OVEN-"FRIED" CATFISH

Growing up, fried catfish was a staple in our house. It's one of my mom's favorite foods, and she must have passed that preference on to me. Another thing my mom and I have in common is that, after we lost weight, we both continued to eat healthier—so we had to drop the deep fryer from the recipe. The seasonings here are a base, but feel free to kick it up with some chili powder, or swap out the parsley for rosemary, oregano, or thyme. With just a little tweak here and there, you can make this recipe your own.

1 cup (100 g) **panko** (Japanese) **bread crumbs**
½ cup (55 g) **plain bread crumbs**
1 teaspoon **kosher salt**
1 teaspoon freshly ground **black pepper**
1 teaspoon **garlic powder**
1 teaspoon **dried parsley flakes**, divided
2 **large eggs**
4 (4- to 6-ounce, or 115 to 170 g) **white fish fillets** (such as catfish)

This also works with tilapia, orange roughy, or cod.

Serves 4

1. Preheat the oven to 425°F (218°C). Place a wire rack on a rimmed sheet pan.

2. In a medium bowl, stir together the panko and plain bread crumbs, salt, pepper, garlic powder, and ½ teaspoon of parsley

3. In a shallow bowl, whisk the eggs.

4. Place the fish on a large cutting board and pat dry with a paper towel. Dip the fish into the egg mixture, and then dredge in the bread crumb mixture, fully coating each piece of fish. Set the coated fish on the rack (or straight on a baking sheet if you run out of room).

5. Transfer the sheet pan with the wire rack and the fish to the oven and bake for 15 to 20 minutes until the bread crumb coating is lightly browned. Use an instant-read thermometer to check that the internal temperature has reached at least 145°F (63°C).

> **CHEAT CODE: If you like your fish extra crispy, broil for 1 to 2 minutes, watching closely, after baking.**

6. Transfer to the wire rack to the counter or a cutting board to cool. Garnish with the remaining ½ teaspoon of parsley flakes.

JERK-STYLE SMOKED CHICKEN THIGHS

2 pounds (908 g) **bone-in, skin-on chicken thighs**

5 tablespoons (75 ml) **avocado oil**, divided

20 ounces (560 g) **Jamaican jerk seasoning** (a dark, liquid seasoning should be used)

2 **yellow bell peppers**

2 **red bell peppers**

2 **orange bell peppers**

Serves 4

I have a good friend who owns a Jamaican seasoning company and tends to send me all sorts of spice mixes. I think it opened my family's eyes to how delicious jerk chicken can be, and this version is a big flavor recipe thanks to the spices, instead of being too reliant on fat and salt. Still, one thing I always want to do is show respect if I'm not familiar with a culture. Jerk chicken is one of those things I have no business speaking about, and I'll admit that to anyone. But a smoker—now that I am familiar with. So, I was really excited to take this flavor profile and combine it with low and slow cooking.

1. Preheat the smoker or oven to 250°F (121°C).

2. In a large mixing bowl, combine the chicken, 2 tablespoons (30 ml) of avocado oil, and the jerk seasoning. Stir to coat well, then transfer the chicken from the bowl to the smoker and cook for 1½ to 2 hours until the internal temperature reaches 165°F (74°C).

3. Meanwhile, heat a large skillet over medium-high heat. Add 3 tablespoons (45 ml) of avocado oil to the skillet and swirl to coat. Add the peppers and sauté for 6 to 8 minutes per side until tender.

4. Rest the chicken for 5 to 10 minutes once off the smoker. Plate as you'd like—pair with rice, make tacos, chop and top nachos. You can even go for a jerk-style pizza (see page 127).

JERK ON EVERYTHING

Swap out the thighs for breasts, wings, or even a whole bird. You'll have to adjust your cook times, but I feel like you learn even more about the complexities of jerk seasoning by trying it on different cuts.

HOUSE AIR FRYER WINGS

4 pounds (1.8 kg) **bone-in, skin-on chicken wings**
4 tablespoons (60 ml) **olive oil**
2 teaspoons (10 g) **garlic salt**
2 teaspoons (6 g) **lemon pepper seasoning**
2 cups (500 g) **barbecue sauce**

Serves 4

1. Preheat the air fryer to 400°F (204°C).

2. Pat the wings dry with a paper towel and place them in a large mixing bowl. Drizzle with the olive oil and stir to coat. Sprinkle with the garlic salt and lemon pepper. Arrange the wings in a single layer in the air fryer basket. You may need to work in batches. Cook for about 10 minutes. Use tongs to turn the wings over. Cook for 10 to 15 more minutes until the internal temperature reaches 165°F (74°C). Transfer to a clean, large bowl.

3. Pour the barbecue sauce over the wings and toss to coat. (How high you toss them is up to you.) For some extra razzle-dazzle, return the wings to the air fryer and heat for 1 minute more. Serve.

This is my recipe for those nights when I'm in the mood for a certain delivery wing restaurant but don't want the deep-fried calories. But then again, baked is just too healthy. It just can't sub in when you get a craving for wings—in my opinion. Now, the air fryer gives you the best of both worlds. You get one step closer to deep-fried, and with the right seasonings. I just love it. So, what's my house flavor all about? Well, lemon pepper is my favorite wing flavor, hands down. But barbecue is what all my kids eat. So, one day I combined them. It's now the flavor I make the most!

OTHER WING FLAVORS

Buffalo: I use a 3:1 ratio of hot sauce to barbecue sauce for a more complex buffalo-style wing. Add the sauce the same way you add the barbecue sauce in this recipe.

Caramelized Shallot Butter (page 22): Put the shallot butter in a mixing bowl still firm. When you add the cooked wings, they'll melt the butter down. Toss them and then back in the air fryer to crisp for just another minute or two.

Smokey Honey Habanero: Try this Spiceology blend or another premade spice blend in place of the lemon pepper and garlic salt in this recipe and drop the barbecue sauce. It works with olive oil, but I find this particular blend, mixed with a few tablespoons of melted butter instead of the oil, is an absolute cheat code.

SMOKED DRUMSTICKS + CRISPY POTATOES

2 cups (480 ml) **cold water**

2 cups (240 g) **ice**

¼ cup (40 g) **kosher salt**

Juice of 1 lemon

FOR THE CHICKEN

2 pounds (908 g) **bone-in, skin-on chicken drumsticks**

1 tablespoon (15 ml) **extra-virgin olive oil**

2 tablespoons (14 g) **Korean barbecue seasoning**

The barbecue seasoning I use is mostly chile flakes and salt, but punched up with sesame seeds, soy sauce powder, smoked paprika, orange peel, and cayenne.

1 cup (250 g) **barbecue sauce**

FOR THE POTATOES

1 pound (454 g) **red potatoes**, halved

1 cup (115 g) **shredded mozzarella cheese**

½ cup (50 g) **shredded parmesan cheese**

2 **garlic cloves**, chopped

½ teaspoon **fresh parsley**, stems removed

2 tablespoons (28 g) **butter**, cubed

½ teaspoon **kosher salt**

½ teaspoon freshly ground **black pepper**

Serves 4

Drumsticks—you have to love them. They are meatier than wings, delicious, and cheaper than thighs and breast. Why aren't there more drumstick recipes out there? This one is my twist on classic barbecue, with smoke and spice in just the right balance. Okay, that said, the potatoes here might just steal the show. I'm not kidding: There are nights when they are gone from the plate faster than the chicken. That is saying something. They have that addictive crunch and remind me in the best way of a mashup of those tacos where the shell is cheese and wedge-cut French fries.

1. To make the brine, first make an ice-water bath for the chicken by combining the cold water and ice in a large stockpot. Stir in the salt and lemon juice to make it a brine.

2. To make the chicken, place the chicken in the brine, cover the pot, and transfer to the fridge. Let the chicken soak for a minimum of 2 hours.

3. When you're ready to cook your chicken, start by preheating the smoker to 275°F (135°C).

4. Remove the pot from the refrigerator and transfer the chicken to a paper towel–lined cutting board and pat dry with extra paper towels. Slather the drumsticks with olive oil and season heavily with the Korean seasoning. Throw the meat on a smoker for about 2½ hours until it reaches an internal temperature of 165°F (74°F). Use tongs to place the drumsticks in a large mixing bowl. Add the barbecue sauce and toss to coat.

WHAT IS A DRY BRINE?

This recipe uses a wet brine, but dry brining is another great way to pack extra flavor into meat. It's super easy, too. Salt is the main ingredient in any dry brine. The way a brine works is that the salt draws moisture to the surface of the meat. The liquid combines with the seasonings and then gets reabsorbed into the meat. At the end of the process, the surface is dry, if you're searing or roasting your meat, you end up with a final product that's crispy on the outside and moist on the inside.

To make a brine, start with a good amount of salt. You can use any salt, but most people, including me, would tell you to avoid iodized salt. Because of the iodine content in regular salt, it'll give your product an off-putting flavor. I like to use kosher salt. If you want more flavors, combine the salt in a medium-size or large bowl with your seasoning of choice. I keep most of my dry brines simple by adding only light brown sugar to the salt. Pat the meat generously on all sides with the salt mixture. Once you're done, wrap the meat in butcher paper. Place a wire rack on a rimmed sheet pan and place your meat on the rack. Let it sit for a few days in the fridge. Every day or so, give it a flip. Do not rinse the meat before cooking.

5. To prepare your potatoes, while your chicken cooks, in a large pot, combine the potatoes with enough water to cover. Bring the potatoes to a boil over high heat. Boil for 15 minutes. Drain and set aside.

6. Preheat the oven to 400°F (204°C).

7. In a large cast-iron skillet, combine the mozzarella, parmesan, garlic, parsley, butter, salt, and pepper. Use tongs to place the potatoes on top of the cheese mixture. Bake for 10 to 15 minutes until the bottom is crispy. Serve with the drumsticks.

BO WELLINGTON

Beef Wellington is something that never really appealed to me, but that's only because I am not a fan of mushrooms. I actually have an allergy to them. Since salmon is one of my favorites, when I went to put my own twist on this famous dish, I went ahead and changed the protein as well as the mushrooms. These days, this is one of my favorite dishes to make. The puff pastry gives you a buttery crunch, the creamed spinach is soft richness, and the salmon brings the middle texture. Oh, and from a presentation standpoint, it's a dish that really stands out—just badass. Once you cut it open and you see that cross section of flaky salmon and creamy spinach, it's a 10/10.

PERFECT PUFF

I use frozen puff pastry. Most brands will be at least 10 inches (25 cm) wide, which you need for this recipe. Using two smaller sheets is possible but harder! Since the puff pastry needs to be ready to go right when the spinach is done, ideally, thaw it the night before. If you did not, now is a good time to get it out of the freezer and put it on the counter. You will need to keep your eye on it, though. If it gets too warm, the butter will start to melt and you won't get that perfect puff.

1 (8- to 10-ounce, or 225 to 280 g) **salmon fillet**
  For flavor, thickness, and a succulent texture, the loin cut of the salmon works best.
1½ tablespoons (18 g) **SPG** (see page 17), divided
2 cups (480 ml) **heavy whipping cream**
1 cup (2 sticks, or 226 g) **salted butter**
1 recipe **Easy Roasted Garlic** (page 25), cloves separated from the oil, or store-bought
4 cups (120 g) **fresh spinach**
All-purpose flour, for dusting
1 sheet (8- to 10-ounce, or 225 to 280 g) **puff pastry**, thawed
2 cups (480 ml) **milk** and **2 large eggs**, whisked thoroughly

Serves 4

1. Preheat the oven to 400°F (204°C).

2. Carefully remove the skin (if applicable) from the salmon and season it with 1 tablespoon (12 g) of SPG. Place the salmon in the fridge while you prepare the rest of the recipe.

3. In a small saucepan over medium-low heat, combine the heavy whipping cream, butter, and roasted garlic cloves. Cook until everything is melted and well combined, about 3 to 4 minutes, then add the spinach and remaining ½ tablespoon (6 g) SPG. Cook for 1 to 2 minutes. Remove from the heat.

4. Coat a clean work surface with a dusting of flour. Lay out one sheet of puff pastry and roll it lightly to remove any seams. Create a layer of the garlic spinach mixture in the center of the pastry the same size as your salmon fillet. Carefully lay the chilled salmon on top of the spinach mixture, with the "top" of the loin facing down.

5. Pull the sides of the puff pastry to cover the salmon going north to south, then east to west, to ensure proper coverage in wrapping. The puff pastry should easily cover the salmon with extra to have substantial overlap—if you have too much extra pastry, cut away any that is more than about a ½ inch (1 cm) overlapping.

6. Flip your Wellington over (so the smooth side is up, hiding the creases underneath) while transferring it to a nonstick baking sheet immediately. The less you handle the puff pastry, the better the finished product will be.

7. Using a sharp knife, crosscut the puff pastry without slicing deep enough to cut the salmon. Brush the pastry with the egg wash, making sure to completely cover the puff pastry.

8. Bake for 20 to 25 minutes, or until the top begins to brown. Let cool for a minimum of 10 minutes and serve!

Breakfast for Dinner

I grew up as an only child, and my dad would make me breakfast every morning. Once I had my own kids, at first, I tried to do the same thing. When my kids were little, it was pretty easy. But as my kids got older, and they all had different wake-up times and schools, nobody was ready at the same time. By Wednesday or Thursday, though, we all craved those classic breakfast foods. Here's the good news: Scrambles, cloud eggs, French toast nachos, you name it . . . they all taste just as good at the dinner table.

PEP 'N' EGG SCRAMBLE ON TOAST

It's cliché to say breakfast is the most important meal of the day, but you can't deny there are some foods that really set the tone for the day. So, as much as I like eggs on toast, I give myself extra credit if I can work in a vegetable, too. That's what makes this recipe work great no matter when you eat it: protein and vitamins. Speaking of, did you know if you compare equal amounts of red bell pepper and an orange, you'll find that the bell pepper has almost three times as much vitamin C?

2 **red bell peppers**
8 **slices brioche bread**
1 tablespoon (15 ml) **olive oil**
8 **large eggs**
1 cup (120 g) finely **grated cheddar cheese**
1 teaspoon **flaky salt**
¼ cup (16 g) chopped **fresh parsley**

Serves 4 to 6

1. Using a sharp chef's knife, cut off the top and bottom of the red bell pepper (see page 96). Make one cut going down the side of the pepper. Insert your knife in the cut you just made. The bottom of the pepper should be facing you and the pepper should be lying on its side on the cutting board. Cut into the pepper, turning the pepper with your other hand as you do. This allows you to remove the core in one fell swoop. The skin side is going to be harder to cut than the inside, so flip the pepper, skin-side down. Cut the pepper into ¼-inch (6 mm) strips, slicing top to bottom.

> **CHEAT CODE: When slicing the bell pepper, glide your knife across it. That way, the knife will never touch the cutting board, and you will extend the life of your knife.**

2. Next, drop the brioche slices in the toaster.

3. Heat a large skillet over medium-high heat. Pour the oil into the hot pan and swirl to coat. Then, add the sliced peppers and cook, stirring often, for 5 to 7 minutes until the peppers are charred and tender.

4. As the peppers cook, crack the eggs into a bowl and beat well using a fork. Once the peppers are charred and tender, add the eggs to the skillet. Cook for 3 to 5 minutes until the eggs are set.

5. Split the egg-pepper mixture across the pieces of toasted brioche. Sprinkle with cheese, flaky salt, and parsley and serve.

VEGGIE BROTH

Tops and bottoms of red bell peppers, onions, carrots . . . nearly any vegetable, even broccoli stalks. These are all great for veggie broth. Start keeping a gallon-size resealable plastic bag in the fridge for veggie scraps. When the bag is full, put the scraps into a large stockpot and add enough water to cover. Simmer over low heat for 4 to 10 hours. The longer you let the broth simmer, the richer the flavor will be. Add your favorite herbs and a skosh of salt to taste for an extra level of flavor.

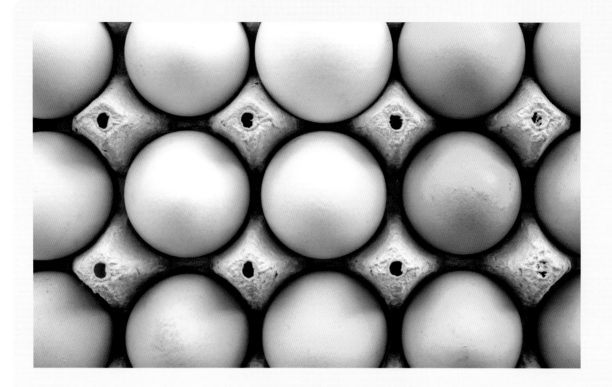

FREE RANGE, CAGE-FREE, PASTURE RAISED?

Eggs can be confusing these days. There are all sorts of things to consider—from size to how the chickens are treated.

Grade A eggs are normally what you'll see in the grocery store—think conventional eggs. If the package doesn't have anything but "Grade A" on it, you can assume the hens are in cages.

Cage-free sounds good, and it is better for the chickens than just Grade A as the hens aren't kept in cages, but those words have little to do with the amount of space they are kept in or any effects on their diet.

Free-range eggs, on the other hand, come from hens that are allowed to roam outside, so that would be even better than cage-free for the chickens.

Pasture raised is a meaningful term (at the time of writing) because it defines both space and feed with some rules. It means each hen is given at least 108 square feet (10 sq m) of roaming room and fed a pastured diet, which is all natural. Unless you see this term, it probably means the hens that laid the eggs are fed a diet that mainly consists of corn and soy.

Does any of this matter for nutrition? There are many opinions on this, but one study that stood out to me was from Pennsylvania State University's College of Agricultural Sciences: They compared the eggs of the commercial hens and pastured hens and found that the eggs from pastured hens had twice as much vitamin E, long-chain omega-3 fats, and more than double the total of omega-3 fatty acids.

Here's my thought: Regardless of the numbers, I don't want eggs from upset or stressed hens. I want some nice, relaxed hens laying my eggs.

COME TO THE TABLE POTATO SKILLET

6 **slices center-cut bacon**, chopped
3 large **russet potatoes**, diced
¼ cup (60 ml) **avocado oil** (optional)
1 cup (115 g) shredded **Colby-Jack cheese**
4 **large eggs**
½ teaspoon **kosher salt**
1 teaspoon freshly ground **black pepper**
½ cup (50 g) **scallions** (green part only), thinly
    sliced on the diagonal

Serves 4

When you're raising teens, time becomes extra precious. They're busy. You're busy. It's hard to get quality time. When most of my kids were teens, I used this recipe as a cheat code to get more time some nights. The beauty is it's in one pan and it's fun to make. Ideally, you get together not just cooking, and not just at the table, but all sitting around the same large skillet eating together. (Yes, yes, I know this is a dinner book, but we love this recipe for Saturday brunch as well!)

1. First, add the chopped bacon to a cold skillet and cook over medium-high heat, stirring often, until crispy, about 10 minutes. Transfer the bacon to a paper towel–lined plate, leaving the grease in the pan.

2. Put the potatoes in the skillet and stir—you want all the potatoes to be glossy and covered in grease. If they're not, add up to ¼ cup (60 ml) of avocado oil. Turn the heat to medium-high and cook until the potatoes are golden brown and soft, 10 to 15 minutes.

If you have access to thick-cut deli bacon, you'll get enough grease without needing the avocado oil.

3. Keep the skillet on the stove and reduce the heat to medium. Crack your eggs in the center of the skillet. If you want to make a nice shape, use an egg mold. Cook until the egg whites are set, about 5 minutes.

CHEAT CODE: If you don't have an egg mold, take a spoon and move it around in a circle until a small well develops. The reason for this is to keep the egg intact—not spread across the entire dish if you drop it on top. From a presentation perspective, you want to show off the egg and potatoes separately.

4. While the eggs cook, sprinkle the cheese and the bacon evenly on top of everything. Sprinkle with salt and pepper. Remove from the heat when the eggs are done, garnish with scallions, grab a hot pad and your family, and gather around the table to eat directly out of the skillet, being careful not to burn yourself on the hot pan.

FRENCH TOAST BREAKFAST NACHOS

8 (10-inch, or 25 cm) **flour tortillas**
1 cup (240 ml) **avocado oil**
¼ cup (28 g) **ground cinnamon**
½ cup (120 g) packed **brown sugar**
8 **breakfast sausage links**
8 **large eggs**
1 teaspoon **olive oil**
2 cups (230 g) **shredded cheddar cheese**
1 cup (320 g) **maple syrup**
¼ cup (25 g) **scallions** (green part only), thinly sliced on the diagonal

Serves 4

My number-one breakfast item growing up was French toast. When my family and I moved to Texas, tacos and nachos became a big part of our diet. So, this is all that coming together. I love serving this as a big brunch appetizer or as part of a breakfast charcuterie board. After a fun night out with the gang, this also makes for a great wake-up and recharge meal.

Okay, yes, it does take time, but frying your own tortillas is worth it because it's a total flavor and texture game changer compared with the grocery store version—and you can salt them to taste.

1. Start by cutting your tortillas into eighths to make chips. Pour the avocado oil into a large skillet and turn the heat to high. Heat the oil to 350°F (180°C). Keeping the oil temperature steady, and working in batches, gently place the chips into the hot oil and cook for 1 to 2 minutes until crispy and golden brown. Use a slotted spoon to transfer the chips to a large bowl. Sprinkle with cinnamon and brown sugar. Toss to coat.

2. Next, place your cinnamon sugar–coated chips on four plates, dividing them evenly.

3. Cook the breakfast sausage links per the package instructions. Chop and set aside.

4. Crack the eggs into a large bowl and whisk with a fork.

5. In a medium-size nonstick skillet over medium heat, heat the olive oil, swirling to coat the skillet. Pour in the eggs. Cook, stirring often, until the eggs are cooked to your liking (I like soft scrambled). Set aside.

CHEAT CODE: If you like soft scrambled eggs like I do, when the eggs are halfway finished, remove them from the heat. The residual heat from the pan will continue to cook the eggs and you reduce the risk of overcooking them while assembling your nachos.

6. To assemble your nachos, top the chips with the cheese, the breakfast sausage, maple syrup, and scrambled eggs, and finish with scallions, splitting the topping ingredients evenly among the plates.

FANCY FRENCH TOAST

2 cups (480 ml) **milk**

4 teaspoons (11 g) **cornstarch**

2 teaspoons **ground cinnamon**

2 teaspoons **sugar**

4 tablespoons (½ stick, or 56 g) **butter**, divided

1 loaf **croissant bread**, sliced into 1-inch (2.5 cm)-thick pieces (you want about 8 slices)

1 cup (320 g) **maple syrup** or **Fruit-Infused Syrup** (page 101)

Serves 4

I grew up eating French toast with a classic crust, meaning dipped in a light egg and milk mixture, then seared in a pan. One major component of French toast is butter. It's what creates that savory crunchy outer. Croissant bread is layered with butter. So, how can we maximize butter flavor? Swap croissant bread for regular bread. Now, croissant bread is airier, which is why I add the cornstarch. It helps get a more consistent crunch, like the French toast you know and love.

1. In a large bowl, whisk the milk, cornstarch, cinnamon, and sugar to combine.

2. Heat a large nonstick skillet over medium heat. Add 1 tablespoon of butter to melt and swirl to coat the skillet.

3. Working in batches, dip the bread slices in the milk mixture and place in the buttered pan. Cook on both sides until golden brown, 3 to 5 minutes per side. Add more butter to the skillet, as needed. Transfer the cooked French toast to a plate. Repeat with the remaining bread. Serve with maple syrup and any remaining butter.

FRUIT-INFUSED SYRUP

1 cup (320 g) **real maple syrup** (Michele's is my go-to brand, especially butter pecan)
½ cup (73 g) **fresh blackberries**
½ cup (63 g) **fresh raspberries**
¼ cup (25 g) **pecan halves**
1 teaspoon **sugar**
1 teaspoon **ground cinnamon**

Makes about 1½ cups (354 ml)

Okay, this was inspired by a popular pancake chain restaurant. They always had myriad syrup options for pancakes, which inspired me to go beyond maple at home. The problem arose when I researched those syrups to see what was in them—so many additives and preservatives. I found the same thing at the grocery store for any syrup that wasn't pure maple. The whole point of making your own is you can start with a high-end base syrup and actual fruit. You eliminate the additives and preservatives, and you get a better flavor.

1. In a medium saucepan, combine the maple syrup, blackberries, raspberries, pecans, sugar, and cinnamon. Turn the heat to high and cook, stirring with a wooden spoon. Use your spoon to smash the berries against the bottom or sides of the pan to release their juices. Once the mixture reaches a boil, reduce the heat to medium and simmer the syrup for 5 to 7 minutes, or until reduced by about half.

> **CHEAT CODE:** The goal here is to get back to the original syrup consistency. The amount of cooking needed to reduce will vary based on the water content of the fruit. The natural sugars in the fruit will caramelize while they cook and help thicken it as well.

2. Remove the syrup from the heat and serve over waffles or pancakes or anything you like. Refrigerate in an airtight container for up to 2 weeks.

This recipe works with all kinds of fruit. I've tried strawberries, peaches, and pineapple. The pineapple is sweeter and tangier than the others, but they were all good. You may need to adjust how much fruit you use, depending on the type you are using. For instance, with the pineapple, I found that ½ cup (80 g) of fruit provided a strong flavor. Any more might have been overwhelming. If you want to use canned fruit instead of fresh fruit, consider rinsing or draining some of the juice from the can so the mixture isn't too watery or sugary. I have not tried frozen fruit, because I worry about the amount of moisture it would add.

BOILED BACON

16 slices center-cut bacon

Serves 4 to 5

When you're looking for maximum crunch, try boiled bacon. It sounds odd, but this cooking method results in extra-crispy bacon. While bacon has a high amount of sodium, turkey bacon is often thought to be a great replacement but actually has almost as much sodium. I am not a fan. But if you want to reduce sodium in regular bacon, boiled bacon is the way to go. The water will absorb some of the salt, and it will evaporate out in the boil.

Heat an oversize skillet over medium-high heat. Add the bacon to the skillet and pour in enough water (usually 1 to 2 cups, or 240 to 480 ml) to cover the bacon. Increase the heat to high, cover the skillet, and cook until the water evaporates, about 20 minutes. Reduce the heat to medium and cook for 2 to 3 minutes until crispy.

THE BEST BACON

When buying bacon, center cut should be your go to. The difference between center cut and the other types of bacon is center cut has a more balanced fat-to-flesh ratio. Now, if you want to go even further, Duroc pork is the "A5" of the pork/bacon world (see page 46). If you can find Duroc bacon, this is the ultimate cheat code. Chances are, it's not in the fridge or freezer at your grocery store—it's at the meat counter. This bacon is thicker and juicer, and cooks much better than the packaged stuff.

Note: Just about all bacon has naturally occurring nitrites or nitrates regardless of cut. So, when you see "no nitrates added" on bacon, this means there were no additional nitrates added.

ONE-TAKE BREAKFAST TACOS

2 tablespoons (28 g) **salted butter**, divided
8 (6-inch, or 15 cm) **chipotle-flavored tortillas**
8 **large eggs**
½ teaspoon **kosher salt**
½ teaspoon freshly ground **black pepper**
¼ cup (28 g) **shredded fontina cheese**, divided
1 tablespoon (15 ml) **chili oil**

Serves 4 (2 tacos per person)

This recipe was inspired by the viral trend of putting tortillas in a pan, adding egg, and making that all-in-one taco. This is my version. The beauty is the crispy taco gives you an awesome crunch and the runny yolk brings it all together. I do want to say this is great for a crowd—start with a base of just taco and egg, but then make a toppings bar. Have some cooked breakfast meat, herbs, vegetables . . . chipotle-flavor tortillas add a little extra complexity to this dish, but any tortilla will do.

Heat an extra-large skillet over medium-high heat. Add 1 tablespoon (14 g) of butter to melt and swirl to coat the skillet. Place 2 tortillas in the skillet and cook for 30 seconds. Flip. Crack an egg on top of each tortilla and sprinkle with salt and pepper. Top each egg with 1 tablespoon (7 g) of cheese. Reduce the heat to medium-low and cook for 2 to 3 minutes until the egg is set. Transfer to plates and drizzle with chili oil. Repeat with the remaining butter, tortillas, eggs, spices, cheese, and chili oil until you have 8 open-face tortillas. Fold and eat.

GET STEAMY

In this recipe, it's all about texture. You want the tortilla crispy, but the egg needs to cook and the cheese needs to melt. If you are struggling with this, steam to the rescue. To add extra moisture, form a 1-inch (2.5 cm)-diameter cup from aluminum foil. Pour ¼ cup (60 ml) of water into the foil cup and place it inside the skillet. This will create extra steam inside the pan.

EGG WHITE BITES

If you're busy in the morning and you don't have time to make breakfast but still want to eat healthy, make these bites in big batches at the beginning of the week. The beauty is that your options are unlimited both when it comes to what you load them with and what you top them with. This recipe is what I landed on as my favorite: I could eat it every morning. It's loaded with fresh veggies, and you get a big punch of flavor from the chili oil and parsley.

If your muffin tin is coated well with nonstick spray, you can really pack them full of vegetables. This recipe is moderate as is. You could almost double everything but the egg white.

Nonstick Cooking Spray (page 18)
  or store-bought
1 **green bell pepper**, diced
1 cup (30 g) **fresh spinach**
1 **Roma tomato**, diced
½ cup (58 g) shredded **Colby-Jack cheese**
1 (16-ounce, or 454 g) container **liquid egg whites**
2 tablespoons (30 ml) **chili oil**
2 tablespoons (8 g) chopped **fresh curly parsley**
2 tablespoons (16 g) **toasted sesame seeds**

Makes 12 egg bites

1. Preheat the oven to 350°F (180°C).

2. Coat a standard 12-cup muffin tin with cooking spray. Add the bell pepper, spinach, tomato, and cheese to the coated muffin cups, dividing evenly among the cups. Pour the egg whites over the veggies until each cup is full.

3. Bake for 20 minutes or so until the eggs are set.

4. Top with chili oil, parsley, and roasted sesame seeds and enjoy! If making ahead, store the bites in an airtight container for up to 5 days.

PEPPER PROCESSING

I love cooking with bell peppers. They're one of my favorite fruits (seeds on the inside means that although these guys are often used in vegetable-forward settings, they're actually fruit!). Not sure how to cut a bell pepper? Here's my method: Start by trimming off the top, then the bottom, and then cut along the inside edge following the pith. From there, you can slice or dice however you please.

CLOUD EGGS

4 **large eggs**
½ teaspoon **paprika**
¼ teaspoon **kosher salt**
1 tablespoon (7 g) shredded **smoked cheddar cheese**
2 tablespoons (12 g) **scallions** (green part only),
  thinly sliced on the diagonal

Serves 2

Are you ready to serve up a cloud? If you are Team Eggs for dinner and you haven't tried cloud eggs, let's change that. Now, while cloud eggs are known for their fun, cloudlike shape, that look can be deceiving. The eggs whites are so soft up top, but hidden underneath is a crunchy bottom. Then, you add the gooey yolk and you get the best of three worlds for texture. I say make this when you want to show off. Plate it on a charcuterie board and place jams and cheeses all around to really get people talking. Cloud eggs are an absolute showstopper.

1. Preheat the oven to 400°F (204°C). Line a baking sheet with a silicone mat.

2. Separate the egg yolks from the whites, placing the egg whites together in a small mixing bowl and each egg yolk in its own small bowl. Using a handheld mixer or in a stand mixer fitted with the whisk attachment, beat the whites starting at low speed and ramping up to high speed until stiff peaks form.

> **CHEAT CODE: Use a mixer. You do not want to be whisking this recipe by hand.**

3. Spoon the egg whites onto the mat, making four mounds. Make a subtle volcano-like shape by gently pressing the back of a spoon into each mound and moving it around in a circle until a small well develops.

4. Bake for 5 to 6 minutes until the ridges start to turn golden brown. Remove from the oven and drop 1 egg yolk into each well. Season with paprika and salt. Place the eggs back in the oven and bake for 4 to 5 minutes more until the yolks are set.

5. Once cooked, while the eggs are still hot, sprinkle the clouds with the cheese and scallions to serve.

CUSTOM SPICY PAPRIKA BLENDS

Let's talk about paprika. Paprika is essentially dried red bell peppers that are ground up. I like to make mine a little more interesting by grabbing some of those dried-out peppers you see at the grocery store. I snag a bag of those, throw a few in the food processor until they break down into a powder, and then combine that powder with the paprika to give it a little kick.

PAIN PERDU MUFFINS (OR BITES)

Pain perdu is the original name for French toast. Before refrigeration was invented, when bakers had bread left over from the previous day, they would rehydrate it in milk. Now, with modern French toast, you customarily dip it in liquid. If the French toast flops in the middle, it's too soaked. So, how do you avoid that? Well, if you start out with stale bread, the liquid rehydrates it instead of making it soggy. So, this keeps in tradition with the spirit of pain perdu. Why muffins? Well, I think of this as the burnt-end version of French toast. With little bites, it's essentially all ends. Combine the ends in a tin and you end up with French toast burnt-ends muffins.

FOR THE FRENCH TOAST

4 **large eggs**
1 cup (240 ml) **milk**
¼ teaspoon **ground cinnamon**
½ teaspoon **brown sugar**
½ teaspoon **granulated sugar**
1 teaspoon **vanilla extract**
4 cups (140 g) **stale bread cubes**
Nonstick Cooking Spray (page 18) or store-bought

FOR THE ICING

1 cup (112 g) **powdered sugar**, plus more as needed
2 tablespoons (30 ml) **milk**

Serves 4

1. To make the French toast, place an oven rack in the center position and preheat the oven to 375°F (191°C).

2. In a large bowl, whisk the eggs, milk, cinnamon, brown sugar, granulated sugar, and vanilla to blend. Add the bread cubes to the bowl and toss to coat evenly.

3. Coat 2 standard (12-cup) nonstick muffin tins with cooking spray. Place a scoop of the bread mixture into each muffin cup.

4. Bake on the center rack until golden, bubbly, and majestic, about 20 minutes.

5. To make the icing, start with 1 cup (112 g) of powdered sugar in a medium-size bowl. Add the milk and stir until you reach a glaze-like consistency. Drizzle the icing over the French toast bites.

CHEAT CODE: Add 1 teaspoon freshly squeezed lemon or lime juice to the icing for a tangy glaze.

THE LOST TOAST

Ironically enough, French toast isn't even French. The fourth-century CE *Art of Cooking* by Apicius actually references bread as "the lost bread." Back in Rome, they didn't want to waste any bread so they just took the stale bread and soaked it in some milk. Fast-forward all the way to 1871. *The Encyclopedia of American Food and Drink* contains the first mention of the term *French toast*. However, depending upon who was cooking it, they were calling it "German toast," "French toast," whatever. It was the Americans who said, "Let's call it French toast."

THE UN-FRITTATA

When I was losing weight, I ate a lot of eggs. Scrambled and fried eggs get old quick when you're eating a ton of them. This recipe helped me pack in some extra flavor in a healthy way. It was also a great time-saving trick because I could make it up one day and then eat it for a few days.

The thing with this is, it's not a frittata. It was inspired by my mom's quiche. To this day, she overnights me quiches on my birthday because I just can't duplicate hers. This is a crustless version, but it's not a frittata because of the sour cream. I think you can make this look so good. you can serve it to a crowd and have it be impressive, but it's also great to cook once and eat all week on your own!

8 **large eggs**
¼ cup (60 g) **sour cream**
1 **small red onion**, diced
1 **red bell pepper**, diced
1 cup (30 g) **fresh spinach**
1 teaspoon freshly ground **black pepper**
1 tablespoon (4 g) **fresh dill**, chopped
1 teaspoon **chili oil**
½ cup (58 g) **shredded cheddar cheese**

Serves 4

1. Preheat the oven to 400°F (204°C).

2. In a large mixing bowl, whisk the egg and sour cream to combine. Add the onion, bell pepper, spinach, pepper, and dill and whisk again until combined. Pour the egg mixture into an oven-safe cast-iron skillet. Drizzle with the chili oil and sprinkle the cheese over the top. Bake for 20 to 25 minutes until cooked through and firm. Test by inserting a toothpick into the center, which should come out clean. Serve immediately and store any leftovers in an airtight container for up to 1 week.

> **CHEAT CODE: You might think I made a mistake here and meant to top with the chili oil after baking. That's not the case. By adding the chili oil before baking, the oil is heavier than the egg, so it will drop down and combine with the egg. When the egg solidifies, you'll get chili oil in every bite— not just as a topping.**

PUFF PASTRY BREAKFAST BOATS

1 (17.3-ounce, or 490 g) package **frozen puff pastry sheets**, thawed
2 tablespoons (30 ml) **water**, plus more for the pastry
8 **large eggs**, divided
2 teaspoons **chili oil**
¼ cup (35 g) **ground breakfast sausage**
½ cup (46 g) **sliced bell pepper**, any color
2 teaspoons **extra-virgin olive oil**
½ cup (60 g) freshly grated **Gouda cheese**
¼ cup (45 g) diced **tomato**
1 teaspoon **dried tarragon**
Skosh (¼ teaspoon) **Cajun seasoning**

Serves 4

A big reason Bo Wellington (page 88) is a favorite for me is the texture and airiness of the puff pastry. I think it can elevate so many different things you cook with. Don't believe me? How about we make breakfast with it? These pastries make for a treat of a breakfast or a great brunch appetizer. Looking for a kid-friendly version? Drop the Cajun seasoning and swap the Gouda for cheddar.

1. Preheat the oven to 350°F (180°C).

2. Unfold the puff pastry on a large cutting board. Using a pizza cutter or sharp knife, slice the pastry into 8 rectangles that are 5 inches (13 cm) wide.

3. Using a pastry brush, brush one puff pastry rectangle with water and layer a second piece of puff pastry on top; the water should adhere the puff pastry pieces together. Trim the edges to make both pieces even, if necessary. Repeat with the remaining puff pastry pieces. Place the puff pastry stacks on a rimmed sheet pan.

4. In a small bowl, use a fork to whisk 2 eggs and the water to create an egg wash. Brush the egg wash on top of the pastry stacks. Bake for 20 minutes, or until golden. Remove from the oven and leave the puff pastry on the pan to cool. Leave the oven on.

5. Meanwhile, in a large skillet over medium-high heat, heat the chili oil. Add the ground sausage and cook, stirring often, until slightly browned, about 5 minutes. Add the bell pepper and cook until crisp-tender and the sausage is cooked through and no longer pink, about 6 minutes.

6. Crack the remaining 6 eggs into a bowl and whisk until well combined. In a medium skillet over medium-high heat, heat the olive oil. Pour in the eggs and cook, stirring often, until set, about 5 minutes.

7. When the puff pastry has cooled slightly, cut a rectangle out of the first layer (don't cut all the way through the stack) of each piece of puff pastry, creating a well large enough to fill with your toppings. Fill each pastry boat with scrambled eggs and top with the sausage and pepper mix. Sprinkle with cheese and return to the oven. Cook until the cheese melts, 3 to 5 minutes.

8. Plate and finish by topping each boat with diced tomato, tarragon, and Cajun seasoning.

AVOCADO TOAST

I love making brunch for my wife, Tee, and avocado toast is one of the things I can make quickly and still impress her. Here's my take on this uber-popular dish: For me, the perfect version is all about nailing the texture. I don't like it when it's so creamy there's nothing to it. On the other hand, you don't want it super chunky. I mash my avocado gently and add some tomato to hit that middle ground.

1 **French baguette**
1 tablespoon (14 g) **butter**
2 **avocados**
½ teaspoon freshly ground **black pepper**
½ teaspoon **kosher salt**
½ teaspoon **garlic powder**
1 **shallot**, minced
1 or 2 **Roma tomatoes**, thinly sliced
1 teaspoon **toasted sesame seeds**

Serves 4

1. Preheat the oven to 350°F (180°C).

2. Slice the baguette into ½-inch (1 cm)-thick pieces (you want 2 to 3 pieces per person) and butter one side of each slice. Place the slices, buttered-side up, on a baking sheet and toast in the oven for 10 to 15 minutes until golden. Remove from the oven and let cool.

3. Meanwhile, remove the pits from the avocados and transfer the flesh to a small bowl. Add the pepper, salt, garlic powder, and shallot. Mash that together with a fork. Spread the avocado mixture onto the toasted side of the cooled bread. Top with sliced Roma tomatoes and toasted sesame seeds.

TEXTURE TIPS

In this recipe I like using a baguette because it has more crunch than standard toast. So, you get a nice bite from that as well. Toasting the bread before adding the avocado mash is optional, but I do recommend it, with a baguette in particular, because otherwise the soft interior of the bread can sag under the avocado.

You're probably wondering why not flip the bread and toast both sides? Well, you want to add crunch up top but not at the bottom, which is why you toast just one side. (And I think a fully toasted baguette can just destroy your mouth!)

CURED EGG

½ cup (100 g) **sugar**
½ cup (80 g) **kosher salt**
1 **large egg yolk**

Serves 1

1. In a small bowl, stir together the sugar and salt. Place half of the mixture in a small food storage container. Add the egg yolk. Top the yolk with the remaining sugar mixture. Cover the container and place it in the refrigerator for 4 days.

2. Carefully remove the yolk from the sugar mixture. Rinse—I suggest you do this by dropping the yolk in a small bowl of water and using your hand to remove it carefully.

3. Preheat the oven to 150°F (66°C). Place a wire rack on a baking sheet.

4. Transfer the yolk to the wire rack and bake until the egg is set, about 2 hours. Store in an airtight container in the refrigerator for up to 1 week.

There are five main tasting senses: sweet, sour, salty, bitter, and savory, or umami. Kikunae Ikeda was a chemist who wanted to find out what gave dashi, a popular Japanese stock, the flavor it had. He looked at the molecular makeup of one of the main ingredients, which was seaweed. He broke that down until he was left with one substance, glutamic acid, and coined the name for its taste as "umami," which directly translates from the Japanese word *umai*, meaning "delicious." I've heard umami described as the taste of beef stock, but it's most often associated with protein like meat and eggs. So, I think the best way to open that umami palate is with a cured egg yolk. For some extra razzle-dazzle, add cured eggs to salads, burgers, or ramen.

Note that you will not be able to taste the sugar and salt in the final product. This is something that can be made ahead. My preferred method to serve this is to grate the egg with a Microplane. It will look like shredded cheese (speaking of, you can slice this and eat it like cheese, right on a cracker . . . but I digress). If it's shredded, I put it on ramen, salads, steaks, burgers, buttered toast, and Avocado Toast (page 113) . . . it will add a layer of flavor to your guacamole as well.

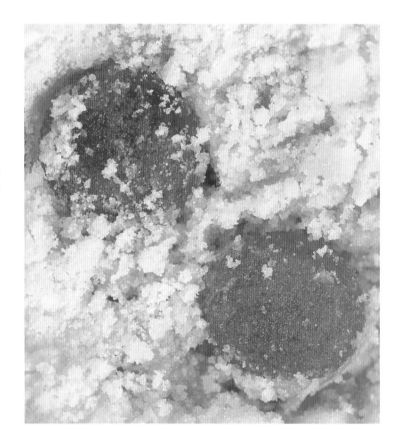

5

Handheld Dinners

Put down the fork and knife. That's right, no spoons either. None of the recipes in this chapter are eaten with utensils unless you really want to be fancy. Seriously though, there are always nights you need portable food. And while I want all my recipes to be fun, it sort of doesn't get more fun than eating with your hands. You just get to grab it, take the bite you want, lick the sauce off your fingers, and go in for more. Keep in mind, the world's first fork may have been made from human bones! You ever wanna eat with your hands or is it just me?

ELEVATED GRILLED CHEESE

8 **slices croissant bread**
3 to 4 tablespoons (42 to 56 g) **butter**, at room temperature
2 cups (230 g) **shredded cheddar cheese**
¼ cup (16 g) **fresh flat-leaf parsley**, chopped

It's said that although many versions of the grilled cheese existed throughout time (think the croque monsieur), the U.S. version, using sliced bread and American cheese, became popular in the 1960s—right after Kraft singles were introduced. You can make a grilled cheese just about any way you'd like, but I prefer to make my standard version with croissant bread, fresh herbs, and shredded cheese. I find that fresh shredded cheese melts evenly and, unlike bagged cheese, does not have additives. Fresh herbs add complexity, and croissant bread really takes the texture to the next level.

1. Depending on the size of your pan, the number of sandwiches you can cook at a time is up to you. For each sandwich, here's what you do: Spread a thin layer of butter on one side of two slices of bread. Place one slice of bread in a large cast-iron skillet, butter-side down, and top it with cheese and parsley. Top with the second piece of bread, butter-side up.

2. Now is when you turn your burner to medium heat and add a lid. Cook the sandwich for 3 to 4 minutes until golden brown. Flip. Cook for 2 to 3 minutes until golden brown. Repeat with the remaining ingredients until you have four sandwiches.

THE LOW AND SLOW METHOD

No, I am not talking about barbecue. I'm talking about cooking grilled cheese starting with a cold pan (and not just this grilled cheese, any grilled cheese). Why do I turn on the heat after putting the sandwich in the pan? Doing this allows the butter to melt first and seep into the bread, which gives you a deeper crust.

Second, adding the lid adds steam to help along the melting of both the butter and cheese. Normally, when you make a grilled cheese without a lid, you end up pressing it down to help the cheese melt. There is no need to do that with the lid.

Note that you will need to adjust the cook time on the first side of the sandwich depending on how fast your stove burner preheats, and for successive sandwiches.

SEAFOOD PLATTER GRILLED CHEESE

3 to 4 tablespoons (42 to 56 g) **butter**, at room temperature

¼ cup (40 g) diced **red onion**

1 (8-ounce, or 225 g) container **lump crabmeat**, refrigerated

8 ounces (225 g) **medium-size cooked shrimp**, thawed if frozen (tails off, peeled, deveined)
Make sure the shrimp and crab are both cold before cooking or you're going to have to reduce the cook time.

8 **slices sourdough bread**

1 cup (115 g) shredded **mild cheddar cheese**

Serves 4

Okay, my normal grilled cheese may be elevated (see page 120), but I can go further. Picture a seafood platter mashed up with a grilled cheese and that's this sandwich. Real lump crab is nice and soft while the shrimp gives you more of a bite, so it goes well together. I've tried it with all sorts of variations, including imitation crab, but nothing works as well as lump crab with the buttery grilled cheese bite. While expensive, it's absolutely worth the splurge.

1. In a large skillet over medium heat, melt 2 tablespoons (28 g) of butter. Add the onion and cook for 1 to 2 minutes until translucent. Add the crab and shrimp. Cook until heated through, 3 to 5 minutes. Remove from the heat.

2. Depending on the size of your pan, the number of sandwiches you can cook at a time is up to you. For each sandwich, here's what you do: Spread a thin layer of butter on one side of two slices of bread. Place one slice of the bread in the skillet, butter-side down. Add ¼ cup (28.75 g) of cheese and one-fourth of the seafood mixture. Add the second slice of bread on top, butter-side up.

3. Now is when you turn your burner to medium heat and add a lid. Cook for 3 to 4 minutes until golden brown. Flip. Cook for 2 to 3 minutes more until golden brown. Repeat with the remaining ingredients until you have four sandwiches. (See note on the Low and Slow Method, page 120.)

SHRIMP UN-TACOS

Tacos are one of my favorite foods, but I can eat *a lot* of them. Lettuce wraps give you pretty much all of the goodness of a taco—including the crunch—with fewer calories. Romaine lettuce is almost made to be a taco, because it's already curved and has a strong handle at the bottom of a stalk. One thing the lettuce taco lets you do is really load it up without spilling out.

GO GREEK

Greek yogurt has more protein than sour cream, but, just as important, it also has a tanginess that brings out my creativity. In this dressing, I add some lemon, lime, and seasoning to create a flavorful sauce.

FOR THE GREEK YOGURT DRESSING

½ cup (120 g) **plain Greek yogurt**
2 **roasted garlic cloves** (see page 25)
2 tablespoons (8 g) **fresh parsley**, finely chopped
1 teaspoon **olive oil**
1 teaspoon freshly squeezed **lemon juice**
½ teaspoon freshly ground **black pepper**
¼ teaspoon **kosher salt**
¼ teaspoon **smoked paprika**
¼ teaspoon **onion powder**

FOR THE SHRIMP

1 tablespoon (15 ml) **avocado oil**
2 pounds (908 g) **raw colossal** (8 to 12 count) or **jumbo** (21 to 25 count) **shrimp**, peeled and deveined
½ teaspoon **kosher salt**, divided
½ teaspoon freshly ground **black pepper**, divided
½ teaspoon **red pepper flakes**, divided
2 teaspoons freshly squeezed **lemon juice**
2 teaspoons freshly squeezed **lime juice**

FOR SERVING

8 **romaine lettuce leaves**
1 **avocado**, thinly sliced
¼ cup (28 g) **shredded cheddar Jack cheese blend**

Serves 4

1. To make the dressing, in a small bowl, stir together all the ingredients to combine. (The garlic should be so soft you can mash it with a fork and stir it right in.) Set aside.

2. To prepare the shrimp, heat a large skillet over medium-high heat. Add the avocado oil to the skillet and swirl to coat. Now, add the shrimp to the skillet and sprinkle with ¼ teaspoon of salt, ¼ teaspoon of black pepper, and ¼ teaspoon of red pepper flakes. Do not overcrowd the pan. You may need to work in batches. Cook for 2 to 3 minutes. Flip. Sprinkle the shrimp with the remaining ¼ teaspoon of salt, ¼ teaspoon of black pepper, and ¼ teaspoon of red pepper flakes. Cook for 2 to 3 minutes more, then remove the skillet from the heat. At this point, the shrimp should be bright pink with an internal temperature of at least 145°F (63°C). Drizzle the lemon and lime juices over the shrimp.

3. To build the tacos, divide the shrimp and avocado evenly among the lettuce leaves—a.k.a. your "taco shells." Put a dollop, about 1 tablespoon (15 g), of the dressing on each "taco," though feel free to add more and spread it around with a spoon. Divide the cheese among the tacos and serve.

TOP-TIER TOASTED SANDO

Panini, or toasted sandwiches, are one of my go-tos when I need a quick meal but a normal sandwich would just make for a sad dinner. For this particular sandwich, I approached it with a "How can I make every layer flavorful?" mindset. Good-quality ham. Fresh shredded cheese. Perfectly ripe tomatoes. Brioche bread. And for the final layer: a sauce that is easy to make but so insanely good.

Do I have any opinions on presses? Well, yes. I'm a fan of the Toastie Press (which is a vertical-style press). The design is brilliant. Because the sandwich is vertical, anything that drips does not soak into the bread. Now, if you don't have a press of any sort, you can still make great hot pressed sandwiches. Heat a large cast-iron or stainless-steel skillet over medium heat. Add 1 tablespoon (14 g) of butter to melt. Add your sandwich and then compress your sandwich with something heavy and heat-proof such as a heavy saucepan. Flip your sandwich after 2 to 3 minutes, smash again, and cook until the cheese is melty and the bread is golden, 2 to 3 minutes more.

Juice of **1 large lime**
Juice of **½ lemon**
1 (5.3-ounce, or 150 g) container **plain Greek yogurt**
1 teaspoon **Dijon mustard**
8 slices **brioche bread**
1 pound (454 g) sliced **deli honey ham**
1 cup (120 g) grated **extra-sharp cheddar cheese**
1 **small Roma tomato**, thinly sliced
2 tablespoons (16 g) thinly sliced **shallot**
½ cup (40 g) **fresh basil leaves**

Serves 4

1. Preheat a panini press.

2. In a small bowl, stir together the lime juice, lemon juice, yogurt, and mustard. Spread a generous amount on one side of each brioche slice. Add a fourth each of the ham, cheddar, tomato, shallot, and basil to one piece of bread, sauce-side up. Cover with a slice of bread, sauce-side down (you'll end up with a closed sandwich with the sauce on the inside). Repeat with the remaining ingredients.

3. Working in batches, add your sandwiches to the press and toast for 3 to 5 minutes until the bread is golden and the cheese is melty.

> **CHEAT CODES: Use a spatula to compress the sandwich before toasting. If you're making panini for a crowd, set your oven to a low temp and use it to keep the panini warm.**

ENDLESS PIZZA

Just like quesadilla night (see page 42) or my Come to the Table Potato Skillet (page 96), this pizza recipe brings everyone together well ahead of dinner because each person can create their own spin on it. This recipe is one of my favorites, and I have more ideas below, but if you keep these pizza crusts in the house, there's also nothing wrong with making it a whatever-toppings-you-have-in-the-fridge pizza night—especially if you have a protein with big flavor like leftover brisket.

PIZZA PARTY IDEAS

Barbecue Pizza: Brisket or pulled pork + barbecue sauce + cheddar + pickled onions + scallions

Taco Pizza: Ground beef or turkey + salsa + Mexican cheese blend + diced onion, diced tomato, and jalapeños (some people like adding shredded iceberg lettuce right before serving)

Veggie Lovers Pizza: Lots of peppers and sweet onion (like 2 cups) + Alfredo sauce + mozzarella + fresh greens like spinach (added right before serving)

Classic Pizza: Do you even need a recipe? Favorite red sauce + Italian cheese blend as the base + pepperoni or whatever you'd normally order!

1 teaspoon **olive oil**
1 **shallot**, diced
½ cup (75 g) diced **yellow or red bell pepper**
1 teaspoon **kosher salt**
½ teaspoon freshly ground **black pepper**
4 small (8½-inch, or 21 cm) **stone-fired artisan pizza crusts**
1 tablespoon (14 g) **butter**, at room temperature
1 tablespoon (8 g) **sesame seeds**
2 cups (230 g) **shredded mozzarella cheese**
1 cup (244 g) **Alfredo sauce**
1 **Roma tomato**, thinly sliced
1 cup (140 g) diced **leftover chicken** or (200 g) shredded rotisserie chicken
2 tablespoons (30 ml) **balsamic glaze**

Serves 4

1. Position an oven rack in the highest position and preheat the oven to 450°F (232°C).

2. Heat a medium-size pan over medium-high heat. Add the olive oil to the pan and swirl to coat. Add the shallot and bell pepper and season with salt and pepper. Cook, stirring, until the vegetables are slightly tender, 3 to 4 minutes. Keep in mind this is a pizza. It's good for the vegetables to have a little crunch.

3. Now, you're going to take your pizza crusts and butter the edges. Then, sprinkle some sesame seeds on those edges for a slight crunch and a little razzle-dazzle.

> **CHEAT CODE: Melt the butter and then use a basting brush to apply the butter to the crusts' edges.**

4. For each pizza, scatter ¼ cup (28.75 g) of mozzarella over the nonbuttered part of the crust and top each with ¼ cup (61 g) of Alfredo sauce. Add the cooked veggies, tomato, and chicken, dividing evenly. Top each pizza with another ¼ cup (28.75 g) of mozzarella.

5. Working in batches if necessary, place the pizzas on a large baking sheet and bake for 7 to 9 minutes, or until the cheese melts. Drizzle the pizza with the balsamic glaze while still hot.

TURKEY DOUBLE CHEESEBURGERS

2 pounds (908 g) **lean ground turkey**
1 cup (110 g) **plain bread crumbs**
1 **large egg**
2 tablespoons (24 g) **SPG** (see page 17)
4 **brioche buns**
½ cup (125 g) **barbecue sauce**
4 **butter lettuce leaves**
8 **slices deli Colby-Jack cheese**
1 **tomato**, sliced

Serves 4

When it comes to a double cheeseburger, turkey may not be the first meat that comes to mind. That said, this recipe is a great way to enjoy most of what's great about a double cheeseburger but with a leaner protein. Thanks to the egg and bread crumbs, you'll improve the moisture and texture of the patties. Season liberally with good old SPG and then quality toppings do the rest. I like butter lettuce as the texture is softer than romaine and I find it sweeter as well. And if you don't already know about my deep love for brioche buns, I'm shocked!

1. Preheat the grill to medium-high. Line a baking sheet with parchment paper.

2. In a large mixing bowl, combine the ground turkey, bread crumbs, egg, and SPG. Mix until uniformly combined. Form eight equal patties and place them on the prepared baking sheet. Don't overcrowd them! You need to give the patties room to expand.

3. Cover the patties with another sheet of parchment and use another baking sheet to press the meat mixture into ½-inch (1 cm)-thick patties.

> **CHEAT CODE: If you don't have another baking sheet, or if you struggle to press all the patties at once, use a heavy skillet or large heavy-duty spatula to press them individually.**

4. Place the patties on the grill and cook for 5 to 7 minutes per side until the internal temperature reaches 160°F to 162°F (71°C to 72°C). Note with turkey burgers there's a thin line between cooked and overcooked. I recommend taking them off short of 165°F (74°C) and tenting them with aluminum foil right off the grill to carry them over 165°F (74°C) without taking them too far past it.

5. As the turkey burgers cook, toast the insides of both halves of your brioche buns on the grill. Look for the bread to develop a golden hue and char marks. This should take less than 1 minute. Set the buns aside when they finish toasting.

6. To serve, drizzle barbecue sauce on the bottom half of each bun. Stack a lettuce leaf, your first turkey burger patty, a slice of cheese, a second turkey burger patty, another slice of cheese, and a slice of tomato. Drizzle with more barbecue sauce and close the sandwich with the top bun. Repeat with the remaining ingredients until you have four turkey double cheeseburgers.

BOUGIE TUNA FISH

2 (5-ounce, or 140 g) cans **chunk light tuna in water**, drained and rinsed
1 tablespoon (10 g) diced **shallot**
2 tablespoons (8 g) **fresh dill**, finely chopped
1 **sweet gherkin**, finely chopped
¼ cup (60 g) **mayonnaise**
2 teaspoons **furikake**, divided
Juice of ½ lemon
1 tablespoon (15 ml) **olive oil**
1 **baguette**, sliced
1 cup (115 g) **shredded cheddar cheese**

The very first fancy dish I remember pulling off was plain Saltine white crackers topped with tuna with mayo and relish, and melted cheese on top. I would put it under the broiler and serve as an hors d'oeuvre. I was watching a lot of Food Network. My dad had made some tuna fish, and I was focused on presentation and plating. Since then, tuna has been a staple. This tuna fish is a more elevated version, of course. The baguette replaces the cracker, and the tuna itself has a lot more flavor. Swapping out gherkins for the relish gives you more crunch.

Serves 4 as an appetizer

1. In a large bowl, combine the tuna, shallot, dill, gherkin, mayonnaise, and 1 teaspoon of furikake. Add the lemon juice. Stir until creamy and combined.

2. Heat a large skillet over medium-high heat. Add the olive oil and swirl to coat the skillet. Use a medium-size cookie scoop or measure out about 2 tablespoons (26 g) of tuna mixture to make a ball and place it in the skillet. Repeat with the remaining tuna. Cook for 3 to 5 minutes without turning until the bottoms start to crust.

3. Preheat the broiler.

4. Using a bread knife, slice your baguette into 12 slices. Place a mound of tuna on a slice of bread to create a bite-size open-face tuna sandwich. Repeat with the remaining tuna mounds and bread slices. Place the sandwiches on a sheet pan, top each with cheese, and place under the broiler. Watch closely, leaving the door cracked open. Broil until the cheese has melted, about 1 minute. Garnish with the remaining 1 teaspoon of furikake.

TORCH IT

If you have a kitchen torch, skip the broiler and hit each of these sandwiches for just a few seconds to melt the cheese.

COD SANDO

2 pounds (908 g) **skinless cod loins**
½ cup (48 g) **lemon pepper seasoning**
10 tablespoons (140 g) **salted butter**, divided
Grated zest of 2 oranges, divided
4 **rosemary sprigs**
3 or 4 (4-count) packages **Hawaiian rolls**
½ cup (60 g) freshly grated **aged Gouda cheese**
1 cup (56 g) **broccoli sprouts**
Hot sauce, for serving (optional)

Serves 4

This is straight up inspired by a steak katsu sandwich. But cod, by nature, is a bit bland to me. Turn that downside into a benefit: It is a fish you can load up with flavor. Don't be afraid to heavily season cod. In fact, I use cod when I'm testing out new spices and seasonings because the flavor is so one-dimensional you can identify what the spices bring much more easily. The seasoning mix you'll find here is one of my favorites. Lemon pepper along with rosemary gives you a complex base. Adding the orange zest gives you the additional aromas and flavors of the oils (feel free to swap orange for lemon or lime zest).

1. Using a sharp knife, cut the cod loins into ¾-inch (2 cm)-wide pieces. Season both sides of each piece with lemon pepper. Set aside.

2. In a medium-size heavy-bottomed skillet over medium heat, melt 4 tablespoons (56 g) of butter. Add the zest of 1 orange. Cook until the butter starts to bubble, then add the rosemary. Stir with a wooden spoon or spatula. Cook until browned butter develops, 3 to 4 minutes.

> **CHEAT CODE: When you smell a pecan-like nutty aroma, you know the butter is ready for the next step.**

3. Add the seasoned cod to the pan and cook until lightly browned, 1 to 2 minutes per side. Feel free to flip and turn the fish in the pan as much as needed to get even browning. Remove the pan from the heat and transfer the cooked fish to a wire rack or paper towels to rest.

4. Preheat the broiler.

5. In a large clean skillet over medium heat, melt 1½ teaspoons of butter. Separate the buns and, working in batches, toast the inside of both the top and bottom bun, adding more butter to the skillet between batches as necessary. Place the bottom buns on a sheet pan.

6. To assemble the sandos, divide the fish evenly among the toasty bottom buns and top each with Gouda. Place them under the broiler for 30 to 45 seconds, or until the cheese melts.

If you have a kitchen torch, use it to melt the cheese instead of the broiler. This typically takes 5 to 10 seconds.

7. Top each sandwich with the sprouts. Slather the inside of the top buns with hot sauce, if you like, and close the sandwiches, sauce-side down.

SALMON FINGERS

Chicken fingers are boring. Okay, I say that having four kids who ate a lot of chicken fingers! To get some variety in my life, I eventually decided to try making them with salmon instead of chicken. Although these have occasionally made it into a taco, usually they get snapped up so quickly after cooking there's no need to figure out a taco or sandwich to put them in. Just eat them like chicken fingers.

1 (2- to 3-pound, or 908 g to 1.3 kg) **skin-on salmon fillet**

3 cups (360 g) **all-purpose flour**

1 cup (224 g) **baking powder**

1 cup (112 g) **cornstarch**

1 cup (100 g) **panko** (Japanese) **bread crumbs**

½ cup (58 g) **ranch seasoning**

1 (12-ounce, or 180 ml) bottle **mineral water**

2 cups (480 ml) **avocado oil**

I like to use mineral water when I'm making this batter. I find that the carbonation makes the batter lighter. This gives you a crunchier, more airy bite.

2 teaspoons **grated lemon zest**

¼ cup (60 g) **spicy mayonnaise** (see Veggie Sandwiches, page 136) or store-bought

Serves 4

1. Slice the salmon fillet horizontally into 1-inch (2.5 cm) strips. Set aside.

2. In a large mixing bowl, stir together the flour, baking powder, cornstarch, panko bread crumbs, and ranch seasoning until combined. Add the mineral water and whisk until the batter is smooth.

3. Fill a wok or large nonstick skillet with deep sides with 1 inch of oil (usually about 2 cups, or 480 ml). Heat the oil until it reaches 350°F (180°C) using an instant-read thermometer.

4. Working piece by piece, and in batches if necessary, use tongs to fully submerge the salmon pieces in the batter and then transfer them to the hot oil—but don't crowd the pan. Each piece should be fully covered with oil. Fry for 5 to 7 minutes until the salmon is crisp and lightly browned on the outside and flaky on the inside (if using an instant-read thermometer, the fish is done when the internal temperature reaches 145°F (63°C). Colorwise, you're looking for a crisp batter that looks just like chicken fingers.

5. Use a slotted spoon or tongs to remove the fish from the oil and transfer to a paper towel–lined plate. Arrange the fish on a large serving plate or tray to serve. Garnish with the lemon zest and drizzle with the spicy mayo.

VEGGIE SANDWICHES

Sometimes, I just have a week where I cooked some barbecue and ate it plus the leftovers, my kids had sporting events, and we ate out a few days as well, and, by the end of the week I'm feeling lethargic and my gut feels heavy. Those are the times when I decide to eat better for a week or two, which usually means dropping the meat. This sandwich is my go-to on those weeks.

The whole point is to pack the sandwich with so many flavors that my mouth is blown away. The butter lettuce and cucumber bring crunch. This texture with soft bread doesn't taste right, so when you toast the bread, you get a similar effect to a grilled cheese. I recommend honey wheat or sourdough bread, or other soft whole-grain breads.

2 tablespoons (30 ml) **extra-virgin olive oil**, divided

8 **slices bread**

¼ cup (60 g) **mayonnaise**

2 tablespoons (30 ml) **chili oil**

¼ cup (32 g) thinly sliced **shallot**

1 **Roma tomato,** sliced

½ cup (46 g) thinly sliced **red bell pepper**

½ cup (60 g) thinly sliced **cucumber**

2 teaspoons **distilled white vinegar**

2 teaspoons **Spiceology Pink Peppercorn Lemon Thyme Rub**

You can replace the Spiceology rub with a standard lemon pepper seasoning with the addition of a small amount of fresh lemon zest and an herb like dried thyme, rosemary, or parsley.

8 **butter lettuce leaves**

Serves 4

1. Heat a medium-size skillet over medium-high heat. Drizzle in 1 tablespoon (15 ml) of olive oil and swirl to coat the skillet. Place the bread in the pan and toast until golden, 1 to 2 minutes per side. You may need to work in batches. Set aside.

2. In a small bowl, stir together the mayonnaise and chili oil until combined. Spread the mayonnaise mixture on one side of each piece of bread.

3. Now, divide your sliced shallot, tomato, bell pepper, and cucumber among four pieces of bread, sauce-side up. Once this is done, drizzle the remaining 1 tablespoon (15 ml) of olive oil on top of the veggies. Splash some vinegar on there, too. Sprinkle some of that pink peppercorn lemon thyme rub over everything and place your butter lettuce on top. Cover with a piece of bread, mayo side toward your veggies. Enjoy!

PB
+
MY FAVORITE HOMEMADE STRAWBERRY JAM

A staple in my house is PB&J, so I have bought just about every jam over the years. That changed when I started reading labels and discovered how many are loaded with less-than-desirable ingredients. After some research and realizing how easy it was to make jam at home, I began to explore different sweet and sour profiles to dial in a perfect strawberry jam (never use store-bought jam again). This is now on repeat at our house.

FOR THE HOMEMADE STRAWBERRY JAM

1 pound (454 g) **fresh strawberries,** hulled and diced

1½ cups (300 g) **sugar**

2 tablespoons (24 g) **pectin**
Pectin can typically be found by the Mason jar section in the grocery store.

Juice of 1 lemon

¼ teaspoon **ground cinnamon**

FOR THE PB AND JAM SANDWICH

2 **slices bread** (I recommend honey wheat)

1½ tablespoons (24 g) **peanut butter**

2 tablespoons (40 g) **homemade strawberry jam**

Makes 1 pint (640 g) jam and 1 delicious sandwich

1. To make the jam, in a medium-size saucepan over high heat, combine the strawberries, sugar, pectin, lemon juice, and cinnamon. Cook, stirring frequently, mashing the berries while you stir, until the mixture reaches a rolling boil. Drop the heat to medium-high. Continue to cook, stir, and mash for 10 minutes or so until the jam thickens. Transfer to a pint-size (480 ml) jar and let cool. The jam will keep in the refrigerator for about 1 week.

2. To make the sandwich, do you really need instructions? This recipe is not about sandwich assembly; it's about the jam!

6

Perfect Bites

The perfect bite series I do is all about how good a single bite can be. Can you win over a person with a single bite of something? The recipes in this chapter are all inspired by that idea. They can knock your socks off with one bite. These recipes are super flexible. Make them as a side. Make them as an appetizer. Or make them as the star to dress up what would otherwise be a leftovers night. Oh, except for the few sweet treats. They are for those nights when dinner might not be terribly exciting so you need a dessert with some razzle-dazzle.

POBLANO RINGS + CITRUS-DIJON SAUCE

FOR THE SAUCE

Juice of 1 lime
Juice of ½ lemon
1 (5.3-ounce, or 150 g) container **plain Greek yogurt**
2 tablespoons (24 g) **SPG** (see page 17)
1 tablespoon (9 g) **dried mustard powder**

FOR THE PEPPERS

1 **large egg**
½ cup (120 ml) **milk**
1 cup (120 g) **all-purpose flour**
1 cup (112 g) **cornstarch**
1 tablespoon (8.5 g) **lemon pepper**
4 **poblano peppers**
2 cups (480 ml) **avocado oil**

Serves 4 as an appetizer or side

Whenever I go out to eat and order onion rings that are thick cut, I feel like the onion-to-batter ratio is off. And when you're frying onion rings, there's a thin line of overcooking the onion as well. On the other hand, I find peppers, like bell peppers and poblanos, are excellent for frying. They're sturdy and don't soften quickly, so a quick trip to the fryer results in super tasty, crunchy bites. With poblanos (or even bell peppers), you can concentrate on the batter and the pepper is much more forgiving. These rings have an intentionally crunchy inside as well as outside, with a little kick of heat. The citrus dipping sauce takes them to another level.

Note: Use the Poblano Rings in other recipes too! They're great as a burger topping, in salads, on top of chili, with Italian sausage, on eggs…you name it.

1. To make that tangy sauce, combine all ingredients in a small bowl and stir to combine. Refrigerate until needed.

2. To make the peppers, first put your egg and milk in a medium-size bowl and whisk it together with a fork. Then, in another bowl, combine your dry ingredients (flour, cornstarch, and lemon pepper).

> **CHEAT CODE: Just like for scrambled eggs, use a fork, not a whisk, to whisk the egg. It will give you a smoother texture and you don't want the extra aeration here from a whisk.**

3. Cut your peppers. First, cut the top off. (See page 94 for what to do with veggie scraps.) Once that's done, go in and carefully cut those seeds and pith out. Lay your peppers on their side on a cutting board and slice them crosswise to make ¼-inch (6 mm)-thick rings.

4. Fill a wok or large nonstick skillet with deep sides with 1 inch (2.5 cm) of oil (usually 1 to 2 cups). Heat the oil to 350°F (180°C).

5. Dip each pepper ring in the egg, then dredge it in the flour mixture. Repeat. Place the rings gently in the hot oil, laying them away from you to avoid splatter. Cook for 2 to 3 minutes. Flip and cook for 2 to 3 minutes more until the batter is golden. Transfer to a paper towel–lined plate using a slotted spoon. Serve while hot with the dipping sauce.

CANDIED SWEET POTATOES

Bacon fat and brown sugar are a match made in heaven, and they make for an awesome sauce. As it turns out, bacon grease, which has a high salt content, also complements sweet potatoes very well. By frying the sweet potatoes in the bacon fat, you get a sweet and savory potato. And since brown sugar is often used to candy bacon, a similar flavor profile happens with this dish once everything comes together.

½ cup (100 g) **granulated sugar**
1½ teaspoons **molasses**
1 teaspoon **honey**

FOR THE SWEET POTATOES

4 **slices bacon**, chopped
4 cups (440 g) cubed **sweet potatoes**

Serves 4

1. Let's start with making your own honey brown sugar. In a medium-size mixing bowl, combine the sugar, molasses, and honey. Use a whisk or handheld mixer to combine until the sugar is evenly colored, 1 to 2 minutes on a medium-low speed, maybe a little longer with a whisk. Set aside.

2. Preheat the oven to 400°F (204°C).

3. Now, let's get started on those potatoes. Take your bacon and place it in a cold cast-iron skillet. Turn the heat to medium and cook the bacon until crispy and the meat is dark red and cooked through, about 10 minutes. Transfer the bacon to a small bowl and set aside, leaving the bacon fat in the skillet.

4. Put your cubed sweet potatoes right in the pan with the bacon fat. Turn the heat to medium-high and cook for 10 to 15 minutes until the potatoes start to brown. Take them off the heat and sprinkle the honey brown sugar mixture on top. Your potatoes will finish cooking in the oven.

5. Transfer the skillet to the oven and cook until the sweet potatoes are soft on the inside and golden on the outside, 15 to 20 minutes. When the sweet potatoes come out of the oven, there will be a nice sauce with them. Plate the sweet potatoes and sprinkle with the bacon.

DIY BROWN SUGAR

Did you know it's easy and quick to make your own brown sugar as long as you have molasses and granulated sugar on hand?

Brown sugar is nothing but regular sugar and molasses. Light brown sugar is typically 3 to 4 percent molasses, and dark brown sugar is anywhere between 5 and 7 percent. (Use 1 teaspoon of molasses for every cup of sugar.) Now, you can completely tweak your own brown sugar and use other sweeteners in addition to molasses. Personally, I like to add honey because molasses can be bitter.

GARLIC-LOVERS' TOMATO SOUP

8 **medium-size tomatoes**, quartered
1 cup (136 g) **whole garlic cloves**, peeled
1 cup (240 ml) **extra-virgin olive oil** plus 2 teaspoons, divided
1 teaspoon **kosher salt**
1 **medium-size red onion**, diced
4 **mini sourdough rounds**
4 tablespoons (10 g) **dukkah**
½ cup (40 g) **fresh basil leaves**, thinly sliced
½ cup (120 ml) **vegan heavy cream**

Serves 4

I started out eating tomato soup at restaurants—yes, sometimes even in bread bowls. But once I realized how simple tomato soup was to make, I started tweaking it. Soon, the razzle-dazzle opportunities emerged. The croutons made here can be used for salads and beat anything store-bought. If you're a garlic lover, like me, develop an extra level of flavor in this recipe by adding an extra ¼ cup (72 g) of roasted garlic to your pot just before blending.

1. Preheat the oven to 400°F (204°C).

2. Start by placing your tomatoes and garlic on a nonstick rimmed sheet pan. Drizzle with about ½ cup (120 ml) of olive oil and sprinkle with salt. Bake for 45 minutes. You're looking for the tomatoes to be charred on the edges. Remove from the oven and let cool at room temperature.

3. While your tomatoes are in the oven, heat a large, heavy-bottomed Dutch oven over medium heat. Add 2 teaspoons of olive oil and reduce the heat to medium-low. Add the onion. Cook, stirring often, until the onion is caramelized, soft, and a rich, deep brown color, about 30 minutes.

4. While that onion caramelizes, let's get started on the sourdough bread bowls. Cut out the middle of the loaf to make a bread bowl. Take the bread you just removed and cut it into ½-inch (1 cm) cubes. Place the bread cubes in a large bowl and drizzle with the remaining ½ cup (120 ml) of olive oil, tossing it all together. Transfer to a nonstick baking sheet and put it in the oven with the tomatoes. Bake until crisp and golden, 10 to 15 minutes.

5. When the tomatoes are done and the onion is done caramelizing, add the tomatoes and garlic to the Dutch oven. Blend using an immersion blender. Transfer the soup to the hollowed-out sourdough bowls. Garnish with dukkah—1 tablespoon (2.5 g) per bowl—basil, croutons, and a drizzle of heavy cream.

IMMERSE YOURSELF

Consistency and texture with tomato soup are key. Placing all your ingredients in a blender and blending into a smooth soup is an option, but I prefer to use an immersion blender because it allows you to better control the texture. Personally, I like a chunkier tomato soup.

GOLD-ROASTED YUKONS

Nonstick Cooking Spray (page 18)
   or store-bought
10 **Yukon gold potatoes**, quartered
1 cup (240 ml) **avocado oil**
1 tablespoon (10 g) **kosher salt**
1 tablespoon (6 g) freshly ground **black pepper**
1 tablespoon (7 g) **paprika**
1 tablespoon (9 g) **garlic powder**
1 cup (115 g) **shredded cheddar cheese**
   (optional)
5 **slices bacon**, chopped (preferably oven bacon,
   see sidebar; optional)

Serves 4

If you know me, you know I love deals—especially on what are normally expensive proteins. But then the planning begins. The next question is often, "I found a deal . . . now, what side am I going to make?" When a roast is on sale and you need a side, potatoes are my go-to.

If you think of potatoes as a "boring" side, that's understandable. They can slip quickly into that territory. The first key to making them more exciting is picking the right ones. I've always though Yukon golds taste like a buttered russet and are some of the most flavorful potatoes. What's more, they have a thin skin compared with russets, making for a great bite when you crisp the skin (as the interior will still be soft). For this recipe, I think the potatoes are fire right out of the oven, but if you need more for your own perfect bite, add the optional cheese and bacon and broil away.

1. Preheat the oven to 400°F (204°C). Coat a roasting pan with cooking spray.

2. Place the potatoes in a large mixing bowl. Add the avocado oil and stir to coat. Sprinkle with salt, pepper, paprika, and garlic powder. Toss the potatoes for even coverage, then arrange them in the prepared roasting pan. Roast for 30 to 35 minutes until tender on the inside and crispy on the outside. You should be able to insert a fork easily in the potatoes when they are done.

3. Optional: Once the potatoes are done cooking, turn the oven to broil and immediately sprinkle the cheese and bacon on top (since we used oven-cooked bacon, some of the residual bacon fat will mix in with the cheese and give you a creamy-textured cheese). Place the potatoes under the broiler for 1 to 2 minutes, or until the cheese is melted with peaks of browning at the top of the cheese bubbles.

OVEN-COOKED BACON

If you want a go-to way to get traditional crispy bacon, look no further than your oven. Preheat the oven to 400°F (204°C). Meanwhile, place a wire rack over a rimmed sheet pan and lay your bacon—I prefer center-cut bacon—out flat on the rack. Pop the bacon into the oven for 15 to 20 minutes, or until done to your liking. As the bacon cooks, the grease falls onto the sheet pan and collects. This is liquid gold. Once the bacon's done, carefully pour the liquid fat into a heat-safe container and store in the refrigerator. I don't bother with straining my bacon grease. I just let it settle to the bottom.

   CHEAT CODE: Make your bacon even better and make it candied with a little brown sugar! See the Sweet Potato Skin Salad with Candied Bacon recipe (page 145) for this irresistible treat. Sprinkle with freshly ground black pepper to add some kick, if you like it that way.

BETTER BRUSSELS SPROUTS

1 pound (454 g) **Brussels sprouts**, halved

1 cup (240 ml) **avocado oil**, divided

2 **garlic cloves**, crushed

1 teaspoon **SPG** (see page 17)

3 or 4 **slices cooked bacon**, chopped (see Boiled Bacon, page 102)

2 ounces (60 ml) **balsamic glaze** (feel free to add more—I certainly do)

Serves 4

Brussels used to get a bad rap, but times have changed. In fact, Brussels eventually became my meal prep company's top-selling veggie. Of course, you have to cook them right. The key, much like the Gold-Roasted Yukons (page 148), is to get a soft inside and a crunchy outside. Once you nail the texture, you can pack in the flavor. This recipe calls for bacon, and I highly recommend the Boiled Bacon (page 102) as it gives you the crunchiest bacon possible without adding quite as much saltiness. The balsamic glaze brings everything together. If you have any friends who still say, "I don't eat Brussels," ask them to take a bite.

1. In a large bowl, combine the Brussels sprouts, ½ cup (120 ml) of avocado oil, and SPG. Toss well to get even coverage.

2. In a large cast-iron pan over medium-high heat, heat the remaining ½ cup (120 ml) of avocado oil until a sprout sizzles if you put it in the pan. Carefully transfer the Brussels sprouts to the pan using tongs or a slotted spoon. Cover with a melting dome or lid, removing the lid and stirring every couple of minutes. Cook until the flesh starts to char evenly without burning, 5 to 10 minutes total.

> **CHEAT CODE: I love to use a melting dome when I'm cooking Brussels sprouts. It allows for a perfect sear but also traps in steam. They're a little hard to find in stores, but you can snag one online pretty easily. If you don't have a melting dome, use a lid or aluminum foil to cover your pan.**

3. Using a large, slotted spoon, transfer the Brussels sprouts to whatever plates you're using to serve. Top each plate evenly with the bacon and liberally drizzle on the balsamic glaze.

WHAT IS MODENA?

You may often see "Modena" on the labels of balsamic "glaze"—from "inspired by" Modena to certified Modena balsamic vinegar. The real stuff is made only in one location in the world—Modena, Italy—and the process is heavily regulated. The vinegar must be produced in Modena or a neighboring area. Trebbiano grapes are the only grapes used, and the vinegar must be aged in wooden barrels for a minimum of twelve years.

SWEET POTATO SKIN SALAD + CANDIED BACON

When I was a kid, as a tradition, my family would go out to dinner at least twice a month. I thought the chain restaurant we went to most had the best potato skins. You got the full flavor of it in every bite . . . it was the one thing I *always* wanted to get. This dish is an ode to that childhood memory with a little spin on it. I like that ginger adds spice . . . taking it to the next level and cutting the richness of the bacon grease. Ginger and garlic, historically, are used fresh, but fried, you get a different dynamic of flavor for each.

SCRAPS OR SPUDS

I first tried this recipe after I made potatoes for my son's football team and ended up with a mountain of skins. Originally these were destined for a compost bin, but then I thought twice about that and experimented with frying them up. I'm all about finding uses for scraps instead of tossing them.

However, if you want to make this recipe but don't have any leftover skins, use the whole potato; just separate the skins, follow the recipe, and then slice the remaining potato into thin fries (I go for ¼ inch, or 0.6 cm) and cook for 5 to 7 minutes until crispy.

FOR THE CANDIED BACON

1 (12-ounce, or 340 g) package **center-cut bacon**
¾ cup (180 g) packed **brown sugar**, divided

FOR THE POTATO SKINS

4 cups (400 g) **raw sweet potato peels**
Avocado oil, for frying
½ cup (57 g) **fresh ginger matchsticks** (1 inch, or 1 cm, long)
¼ cup (40 g) sliced **garlic**
1 teaspoon **kosher salt**
2 teaspoons chopped **fresh chives**

Serves 4 as a side

1. Preheat the oven to 325°F (163°C). Line a rimmed sheet pan with aluminum foil and place a wire rack on the sheet pan.

2. Place the bacon slices on the wire rack so they do not overlap. Sprinkle ½ cup (120 g) of brown sugar over the bacon. Bake for 10 minutes. Remove from the oven and use tongs to turn over the bacon. Sprinkle the remaining ¼ cup (60 g) of brown sugar over the bacon and return it to the oven. Bake for 15 to 20 minutes until the bacon is crispy. Let cool while preparing the sweet potato skins.

3. Place the sweet potato skins in a colander and rinse with tap water. Dry with a paper towel. Set aside.

4. Fill a large pot or Dutch oven with about 2 inches (5 cm) of avocado oil (usually 1 to 2 cups, or 240 to 480 ml). Place the pot over medium-high heat and let heat until the oil reaches 375°F (191°C).

5. Using a slotted spoon, carefully add the ginger to the hot oil. Cook for 1 to 2 minutes. Use the slotted spoon to transfer the ginger to a paper towel–lined plate.

6. Now, use the slotted spoon to carefully transfer the garlic to the hot oil. Cook for 30 seconds to 1 minute until golden, then transfer to the paper–towel lined plate.

7. Use tongs to add the skins to the oil. Cook for 4 to 5 minutes until crispy. Transfer to a paper towel–lined plate and sprinkle with salt. Depending on the size of your pot, you may need to work in batches.

8. Use kitchen scissors or a knife to cut the bacon into bite-size pieces.

9. In a large bowl, combine the bacon, ginger, garlic, and sweet potato skins. Garnish with chives. Enjoy!

MUSTARD PASTA

Now, you've probably had plenty of pasta with cream-based sauces. And, of course, you've had pasta with tomato sauce. But what about mustard sauce? This recipe came about for two reasons: First, I've played with pasta sauces for years. So second, when the mustard binder trend hit in barbecue (see page 54), it got me thinking about using mustard in other recipes in non-traditional ways. It was only a matter of time before I tried it with pasta.

Mustard seeds have a mild, nutty taste to me. When you add vinegar and lemon juice (to make mustard), you have a balanced "base" that can take on a lot of flavor in a pasta dish. In this recipe, I amp up the acid by adding more vinegar, red and white, and then load it with vegetables and fresh herbs.

FOR THE PASTA

2 cups (224 g) **rotini pasta**
2 **fresh ears corn**
2 tablespoons (30 ml) **extra-virgin olive oil**
2 **zucchini**, diced
2 cups (170 g) **broccoli florets**
½ teaspoon **fresh rosemary leaves**
½ teaspoon **paprika**
½ teaspoon **kosher salt**
½ teaspoon freshly ground **black pepper**
Handful **fresh basil leaves**

FOR THE DRESSING

1 cup (240 ml) **extra-virgin olive oil**
½ cup (120 g) **grainy mustard**
1 tablespoon plus 1 teaspoon (20 ml)
    white wine vinegar
1 tablespoon plus 1 teaspoon (20 ml)
    red wine vinegar

Serves 4

1. To make the pasta, in a medium-size pot, cook the pasta according to the package instructions until al dente, then drain.

2. Meanwhile, prepare the corn by removing the husks and silks. Wash. Use a knife to carefully cut the kernels from the cob.

3. Heat a medium-size nonstick skillet over medium-high heat. Add 1 tablespoon (15 ml) of olive oil and swirl to coat the skillet. Add the corn, zucchini, and broccoli and season with the rosemary, paprika, salt, and pepper. Cook for 7 to 9 minutes until the veggies are tender but not mushy. Transfer to a large mixing bowl.

4. To make the dressing, in a medium-size bowl, combine the olive oil, mustard, white wine vinegar, and red wine vinegar. Whisk until combined.

5. Add the pasta to the veggies and pour the dressing over the top. Toss to coat and serve garnished with fresh basil.

ROASTED BROCCOLI + GARLIC CHIPS

1 **head broccoli**
1 tablespoon (15 ml) **avocado oil**
¼ cup (36 g) **garlic cloves**, sliced
1 tablespoon (10 g) **Greek seasoning** (I use Spiceology's Greek Freak Mediterranean Seasoning)
2 tablespoons (12.5 g) freshly grated **parmesan cheese**

Makes 3 servings

When it comes to broccoli, I've always been a fan. I like the taste, and it's high in fiber and vitamin C. My kids' favorite version was broccoli with mild cheddar melted over it. So, I thought, how do you grow up that side dish? Swap the cheese and add crunchy garlic was my answer.

The first time I fried garlic was sort of an experiment. I had hot oil and I had sliced garlic—it wasn't a recipe I found. I was chopping garlic to season the broccoli and, after testing one or two as chips I kept going, and the rest is history. Homemade roasted garlic chips are an absolute game changer, and they can be used in place of fried onions in just about anything. They also go well with Italian dishes.

1. On a large cutting board, use a knife to remove the broccoli florets from the stalk.

> **CHEAT CODE: To keep the florets intact, hold the broccoli upside-down, gripping the stalk, and cut the florets off over a mixing bowl.**

2. Next, in a medium-size pan over medium-low heat, combine the avocado oil and garlic. You do not want the oil to be piping hot; you just want to get a nice simmer. Cook until golden, about 5 minutes. Using a skimmer, transfer the garlic to a paper towel–lined plate, leaving the oil in the pan. Pat with a paper towel to remove excess oil and transfer to a medium-size bowl. Reline the plate with clean paper towels.

3. In the same pan, gingerly lay the broccoli florets in the oil. Hit it with the Greek seasoning. Cook for 5 minutes. Use the skimmer to transfer the broccoli to the clean paper towel–lined plate. Pat with paper towels to remove excess oil. Add the broccoli to the bowl with the garlic and toss to combine. Top with the parmesan cheese.

It's true that for many applications you want to get your pan hot before adding ingredients, but when garlic is the only ingredient in a pan, it needs a slow warm-up. Put it into a hot pan and you're more likely to burn it. That's why it's best to add garlic to the pan before firing up the heat.

CORN SLAW(LSA)

In the barbecue community, regular slaw is common, but if you are looking for something a little more complex than a standard slaw, this will work. What's even better is it can also work on tacos, in quesadillas, on burgers, or even on hot dogs. It's more of a salsa and is also great over salmon and killer on Turkey Double Cheeseburgers (page 130) and Shrimp Un-Tacos (page 124). If you're looking to impress, save your cored pineapple skin and use it as a serving dish.

4 **fresh ears corn**, husks and silks removed
1 **fresh pineapple**, cored and cut into ½-inch (1 cm)-thick rings
2 **limes**
1 tablespoon (15 g) **sour cream**
2 tablespoons (2 g) **fresh cilantro**, finely chopped
¼ teaspoon freshly ground **black pepper**
¼ teaspoon **sugar**

Makes 8 servings

1. Preheat the grill to 350°F (180°C).

2. Place the corn and pineapple rings on the grill and cook for 2 to 3 minutes per side, turning halfway through the cook time. You're looking for good, solid char marks on both the corn and the pineapple. Transfer to a large cutting board and let cool for 5 to 10 minutes. Use a knife to carefully cut the kernels off the cobs. Transfer the corn to a large bowl. Cut the pineapple into bite-size pieces and add to the bowl with the corn.

3. Grate the zest of the limes into a small bowl, then halve the limes and squeeze the juice into the bowl. Stir in the sour cream until well combined, about 30 seconds. To balance the flavor, stir in the cilantro, pepper, and sugar. Pour the sauce over the corn and pineapple. Start with a small amount and add more to taste.

LEMON-LIME FUNNEL CAKES

3 cups (360 g) **all-purpose flour**

3 tablespoons (38 g) **sugar**

1 teaspoon **vanilla extract**

1 teaspoon **baking soda**

1 tablespoon (15 ml) freshly squeezed **lemon juice**

1 tablespoon (15 ml) freshly squeezed **lime juice**

1 cup (240 ml) **almond milk**

2 cups (480 ml) **neutral oil** (such as avocado oil)

¼ cup (28 g) **powdered sugar**

To make this recipe, you'll need a funnel. I've found that auto parts stores have the best ones.

Makes 2 funnel cakes; serves 2 to 4

1. In a large mixing bowl, whisk together the flour, sugar, vanilla, baking soda, lemon juice, lime juice, and almond milk until smooth.

2. Pour the oil into a large skillet and turn the heat to high. Let the oil heat until it reaches 350°F (180°C). Adjust the heat, as needed, to maintain the temperature.

3. Start making the funnel cakes. Carefully hold a funnel 1 to 2 inches (2.5 to 5 cm) above the hot oil. Slowly pour 1 cup (240 ml) of batter into the funnel, moving the funnel around to make designs such as circles or zigzags. Don't be shy about crisscrossing batter over itself so it all connects into one big cake. Once you have enough batter in the oil, fry until deep golden in color, about 75 seconds. Use a slotted spoon to flip the cake and continue cooking another 75 seconds or so until both sides are equally golden brown. Transfer to a wire rack to cool slightly. Dust with powdered sugar while still warm to serve.

4. Repeat with the remaining batter.

I've loved a good funnel cake all my life. My mom often made them from scratch, and I often wondered how she made them. As adults, years ago, my wife and I started a tradition of stopping at any fair we see and buying a funnel cake. Nothing keeps us from a funnel cake (we once stopped to grab one on the way home from a seven-course dinner)!

This recipe is for those times where there's just not a fair in sight. It's good without the lemon and lime, but of course I think these flavors add a little something that's worth trying—and that sets these funnel cakes apart from the tried-and-true classic.

BLUEBERRY DONUT PEACHES

8 **donut peaches**
1 cup (145 g) **fresh blueberries**
4 teaspoons (27 g) **honey**
4 teaspoons (9 g) **ground cinnamon**
2 tablespoons (25 g) **granulated sugar**
¼ cup (60 g) packed **brown sugar**
4 teaspoons (9 g) **powdered sugar**

Serves 4

Donut peaches are called donuts because they are flat and round, just like donuts. The reason these are clutch to me is because of the flavor. They're super sweet and delicious. In this recipe, I double down on the sweetness, turning donut peaches into mini desserts. At my house, we throw these over ice cream, though this is also a great dish to make in bigger batches for a party plate. Oh, and, of course, roll them out for a brunch spread.

1. Hold one of your peaches in your hands and press on the center, pushing out the pit. Repeat with the remaining peaches. Cut the peaches horizontally into 3 rings. Transfer the peach rings to a baking sheet. Fill the centers of the rings with blueberries. Drizzle with honey. Dust with cinnamon, granulated sugar, and brown sugar. Use a kitchen torch to melt the sugar. You are going for a golden brûlée-like crust.

2. Dust with powdered sugar and your filled donuts will be complete!

CHEAT CODE: Feel free to swap the blueberries for raspberries.

LOADED RICE CRISPY

2 tablespoons (14 g) **ground cinnamon**

2 tablespoons (25 g) **sugar**

½ cup (1 stick, or 113 g) **unsalted butter**

1 (10-ounce, or 280 g) bag **marshmallows**

6 cups (228 g) **"frosted,"** a.k.a. **sugar-coated, crispy rice cereal**

Nonstick Cooking Spray (page 18) or store-bought

Chocolate bar and/or candy of choice, for decorating

I often go with one Kit-Kat and one Snickers bar, diced, but you could go with a pack or two of Reese's Pieces or M&Ms, or break up Reese's cups . . . I digress.

Serves 8 to 10 or fewer, if you have hungry kiddos

These treats were something my dad made for me all the time. They are absolutely a childhood memory. But taking his recipe a step further, of course, was inevitable. Now, this is my family's template. By all means, drizzle on melted caramel, dip it in melted chocolate, or add nuts. But the recipe that follows is the classic in our house.

1. In a small bowl, stir together the cinnamon and sugar, then set aside.

2. In a large saucepan over medium-low heat, melt the butter. Then, add the whole bag of marshmallows and let them melt, stirring often. Once the marshmallows start to melt, take them off the heat. Add the cinnamon sugar. Continue to stir until everything is all melty and well combined. Stir in the cereal. It will get sticky.

3. Coat a Bundt pan with cooking spray. Then, it's all about the layers.

4. Add a layer of the cereal mixture to the prepared pan, about a third of the total mix. Then, a layer of your favorite chocolate bar, another third of the cereal, followed by a candy of your choosing, and one final layer of cereal.

> **CHEAT CODE: I recommend using a rubber spatula to pat down your layers. Spritz a skosh of cooking spray on the part you're smashing and the spatula won't stick.**

5. Flip the Bundt pan over quickly and carefully as the treat will fall right out. Slice, and enjoy. Or, if you want more of a single-bite treat, you can continue to cut and break down the slices into bite-size pieces.

The Beverage Lab

Similar to cooking, making a cocktail is as much about the preparation and process as it is the final product. When I was working a corporate career, like many, I'd come home from work and enjoy a drink to unwind. But unlike many others, for me it evolved into a journey where the process of creating the drink was just as enjoyable as the drink itself. I'd start thinking of things like simple syrup: How do you make it better or more interesting? Yes, there's the Old-Fashioned . . . but how do I make it *my* Old-Fashioned? This chapter dives down some of those rabbit holes, and my hope is that you both enjoy the recipes and get inspired to start your own experiments for the little things you can do for a big payoff.

OLEO SACCHARUM

Oleo saccharum directly translates from Latin to "oily sugar," and you can make this with practically any leftover citrus peels—clementines, lemons, limes, or even a combination. What I've learned the more that I've crafted cocktails is that if there's a simple version, there's a more complex version. Simple syrup's complex version is oleo sachharum. I found it by researching the history and origin of simple syrup and I quickly came across oleo. The process intrigued me because it took longer to create . . . not active time. But like barbecue, the time has a payoff. What I noticed about my first batch, which was made with just lemon and limes, was how rich it tasted.

Just respecting the origins of anything, using oleo holds true to some of the original cocktail makers and the art of making drinks. Oleo yields a small amount of a high-quality product. That said, you can adjust the amounts listed . . . if you stray further from the recipe—for example, if you use monk fruit or turbinado—you are going to have to use more sugar. If you're making a cocktail, all you need is, maybe, 1 ounce (28 g) of this stuff and whatever spirit you're going with.

Spirit drinkers: Go for 2 ounces (60 ml) of your favorite spirit, and ¾ ounce (21 g) of oleo, and a few ounces of soda water. Gently pour over ice and stir with a bar spoon. Thank me later.

LEMON-LIME OLEO

7 ounces (200 g, about 2 cups) **lemon and lime peels** (preferably organic)

1 cup (200 g) **sugar**, plus ¼ cup (50 g) more for topping

ORANGE OLEO

7 ounces (200 g, about 2 cups) **orange peel** (preferably organic)

1 cup (200 g) **sugar**, plus ¼ cup (50 g) more for topping

GRAPEFRUIT OLEO

7 ounces (200 g, about 2 cups) **grapefruit peel** (preferably organic)

1 cup (200 g) **sugar,** plus ¼ cup (50 g) more for topping

The yield varies depending on how long you let it sit, the type of sugar you use, and the quality of the citrus. The more oily the citrus, the bigger the yield.

1. Place your peels in an airtight container and cover them with the sugar. Seal the container, give it a shake, then add a skosh more sugar to the top. Put the container in a dark, cool part of your kitchen for about 24 hours.

2. After 24 hours is up, there should be a whole lot of sugar solidified at the bottom of the container, but the oils get extracted, and *that* is the flavor-packed, liquid gold syrup. At this point, I recommend pouring it directly into a glass bottle with no straining. If a few sugar crystals make their way in, they will settle to the bottom. Store in an airtight container in the refrigerator for up to a week. Note that this mixture does get thicker when cold, so feel free to take it back out and let it come back up closer to room temperature before using.

Orange Oleo, page 168

CHEONG

1 **lime** (preferably organic)

1 pound (454 g) **fresh strawberries**, hulled and quartered (preferably organic)

1 pound (454 g) **granulated sugar**

Makes 3 pints (about 400 g each)

Although cheong and oleo saccharum are very similar, there is one material difference between the two. The Latin translation of *oleo saccharum* is "oily sugar," so we're specifically talking about one thing. Traditional cheong actually covers myriad different things—syrups, marmalades, jams, etc. On one hand (the oily sugar hand), we're using the skin, and on the other hand (the cheong hand), we're using the entire piece of fruit.

The other major difference is the time to prep. With oleo, you need to wait overnight, but with cheong, you really need only an hour or two. Keep in mind with cheong, because of the acidity and the fruit combined with the sugar, you're going to get some gas in your container. Because of this, I wouldn't go completely sealed. Cover the top of your container with aluminum foil and poke some holes in it if you wrap super tight. All you're going to do is take your fruit, put it in a container, and top with a generous amount of sugar. That's it!

1. Start by washing all of your fruit. Peel the lime. Set aside the peels. Squeeze the juice from the lime into a small bowl.

2. Divide the strawberries and lime peels among 3 pint-size (480 ml) glass jars. Add the sugar and lime juice in equal amounts to each jar. There's no need to shake or stir. Seal and store in the fridge for up to 1 week.

If you don't have quite enough flavor after 48 hours, let it go longer, to taste. Just keep an eye on it, checking after 12 hours.

UNDERSTANDING OLEOS: THREE RECIPES

I started my journey with oleo making whiskey-based cocktails, but because it is so rich and so complex, I started thinking about getting creative with it. These three short recipes that follow will really let you taste the versatility in different situations.

CITRUS SPRITZ

¾ ounce (25 ml) freshly squeezed **lime juice**
½ ounce (15 ml) **Lemon-Lime Oleo** (page 168)
Crushed ice, for serving
6 ounces (180 ml) **sparkling water**

In a pint (480 ml) glass, combine the lime juice and oleo. Fill the glass with crushed ice and pour in the sparkling water. Stir and serve.

SWEET AND SOUR

2 ounces (60 ml) **tequila**
½ ounce (15 ml) **Grapefruit Oleo** (page 168)
6 ounces (180 ml) **lemonade**
Crushed ice, for serving

In a tall glass, combine the tequila, oleo, and lemonade and stir to combine. Carefully fill to the top with crushed ice and serve.

BO'S SHERBET MULE

2 ounces (60 ml) **vodka**
½ ounce (15 ml) **Orange Oleo** (page 168)
6 ounces (180 ml) **ginger beer**
Crushed ice, for serving
1 **Dried Candied Orange Slice** (page 176)

Serves 1 (each recipe)

In a copper mule mug, combine the vodka and oleo. Pour in the ginger ale, which as it fizzes will gently combine and aerate. Gently stir, if needed. Carefully fill to the top with crushed ice, garnish with the candied orange slice, and serve.

COCKTAIL CHERRIES

1 cup (240 ml) **water**
½ (120 ml) cup freshly squeezed **lemon juice**
1 tablespoon (15 ml) **pure vanilla extract**
1½ cups (300 g) **sugar**
1 **cinnamon stick**
8 ounces (225 g) **fresh sweet cherries**, pitted
¼ cup (60 ml) **Maraschino cherry liqueur**

Makes about 8 ounces (225 g)

I have probably purchased every high-end cocktail cherry on the market. If you have done the same, you know how expensive that can get. In looking at the ingredients, I thought there had to be a way to duplicate this—and without preservatives. This really speaks to my whole thought process. If you're using high-end bourbon, clear ice, oleo, and then you throw in a cherry with preservatives? Nah. Old-Fashioneds and Sidecars are my two favorite drinks. Both historically have cherries in them. So, the cocktail cherry was the first garnish I wanted to create. What's even better is that after you eat all your cherries, you're left with a delicious mixture you can store and use as a cherry syrup in cocktails.

1. In a saucepan over medium heat, combine the water, lemon juice, vanilla, sugar, and cinnamon stick. Cook until the sugar dissolves, stirring occasionally, about 6 minutes.

2. Add the cherries. Bring to a simmer and then remove from the heat. Transfer the cherries to a quart-size (960 ml) Mason jar, cover with the liquid, and let stand, uncovered, until cool. Seal the lid and refrigerate for up to 7 days.

> **CHEAT CODE:** For some extra flavor, freshly grate some additional cinnamon into your liquid mixture before simmering or drop a cinnamon stick into the Mason jar before letting the mixture cool.

PERFECTLY PITTED

To pit a cherry, first remove the stem. Then, use a chopstick to poke the seed out through the bottom of the cherry. This allows the cherries to stay intact.

DRIED CANDIED ORANGE SLICES

Presentation is a critical part of a cocktail. Before you even taste it, you can taste it with your eyes. When you put one of these orange slices on the rim of a glass, it glistens in the light because of the candy coating. Also, they are just good to eat. You can eat the rind and the flesh after the candying process. Good addition to a charcuterie board. This is another recipe with a dual purpose. Our main goal here is to make delicious candied oranges. However, you also end up with some fantastic orange syrup that can be stored and used as an orange simple syrup.

2 cups (480 ml) **water**

2 cups (400 g) **sugar**

2 **large oranges** (preferably organic), sliced into about ¼-inch (6 mm) thick slices

Makes 15 to 20 slices

1. In a saucepan over high heat, combine the water, sugar, and orange slices. Bring to a boil. Reduce the heat to low, maintain a simmer, and cook for 2 hours. You're looking for your orange slices to look like candied jelly. The liquid will be thick enough to coat the back of a spoon (almost as thick as maple syrup).

2. Preheat the oven to 200°F (93°C). Line a rimmed sheet pan with a silicone baking mat.

3. Using a fork or slotted spoon, transfer the orange slices to the prepared sheet pan and bake for 3 to 4 hours or so until you have dehydrated the orange slices. At this point, they should look completely dry with no visible moisture but may still look glossy. Remove from the oven, cool completely, and transfer to an airtight container for up to 2 weeks. (If properly dehydrated, they may last longer.)

> **CHEAT CODE: Do not discard the syrup! Transfer to a glass jar and use it as an orange-flavored simple syrup. Keep refrigerated for up to 2 weeks.**

CITRUS-POMEGRANATE JUICE

2 **lemons**, quartered (preferably organic)

2 **clementines**, peeled (preferably organic)

1 **grapefruit**, peeled and quartered (preferably organic)

1 **lime**, halved (preferably organic)

I use the skin in my recipes. There are different nutrients and flavors in the skin, and I prefer to include them. If you do, too, you may want to purchase organic fruit or wash the fruit well before using.

1 tablespoon grated peeled **fresh ginger**

1 tablespoon **ground turmeric**

½ cup (90 g) **pomegranate arils**

2 cups (480 ml) **water**

Serves 2

Pomegranate has always given me a lot of energy. But pomegranate by itself as a juice is a little strong.

1. In a blender, combine the lemons, clementines, grapefruit, lime, ginger, turmeric, and pomegranate arils. Add 1 cup (240 ml) of water. Blend on high speed for 1 to 2 minutes. Add the remaining 1 cup (240 ml) of water and blend for 1 to 2 minutes more until the mixture is smooth and burnt orange in color.

2. Place a fine-mesh strainer over a large bowl. Pour the blended mixture into the strainer, using a spoon to help separate the pulp from the juice. Don't toss away the pulp! You can use it for either composting or other recipes.

OTHER JUICES

Ginger + Lemon + Honey = I like this when I have an upset stomach or just during cold season as an immune system booster.

Blueberry + Strawberry + Lemon = Blueberry helps hide flavors you don't like, too.

JUICE WITHOUT A JUICER

Let's be honest: A lot of the food that I eat is super rich. (I do healthy-ish, not healthy.) But nutrition is all about balance. On days I eat "poorly," I try to work out more and balance in other ways. Juicing is a way to achieve that balance. Juicing helps make my gut feel clean after brisket or a big steak. Juicing can help through diet transitions as well.

Not everybody has a juicer, though. Maybe you want to try juicing, but without buying a juicer immediately. Using a juicer is easy, but cleaning it? Using a blender, which is more common in most kitchens, you can achieve results that I have found are, in some instances, even smoother than with a juicer. When you use stronger-flavored ingredients like lemon, lime, and ginger, diluting the juice with water allows you to adjust the flavor to your palate. The more you juice, the more you will get used to the flavor, and you may find yourself using less water over time.

BOLD FASHIONED

3 ounces (90 ml) **bourbon** (preferably 100 proof; this also works well with high-proof rye)
½ ounce (15 ml) **Orange Oleo** (page 168)
Crushed ice, for mixing
Clear ice, for serving
1 **Cocktail Cherry** (page 174) or store-bought
1 **orange peel** or **Dried Candied Orange Slice** (page 176)

Serves 1

The Old-Fashioned is probably the most iconic bourbon-based cocktail there is. Just as important, it's my favorite. The Bold Fashioned, as you might have guessed, is attempting to pay homage to the original, but taking a bolder approach to an otherwise classic drink. And, of course, I recommend making it with the Cocktail Cherries on page 174 and Dried Candied Orange Slices on page 176. Why do I skip the orange peel expression at the end? You get that flavor built-in with the oleo.

I like using a Boston shaker for this. Add the bourbon and oleo to the short tin. Load up the tall tin with ice. Gently pour the bourbon and oleo over the ice, secure the Boston, and perform a standard four-point shake for 30 seconds, or until ice cold to the touch. Fill an old-fashioned glass with clear ice, pour the drink over, and garnish with the cherry and orange peel to serve.

> **CHEAT CODE: What is a four-point shake? Think about a rectangle and hit every corner while you shake. One point is your chest, second is away from you, third is back but to your stomach, and fourth is away from you.**

AERATION

A Boston shaker aerates as well as chills and dilutes the drink. When you aerate a drink, the air helps the ingredients mix better and gives the cocktail a lighter feel—especially important when you're working with a higher-proof bourbon. Some people like stirred Old-Fashioneds, but I find them syrupy. I do not recommend double straining this drink as I like the froth from the shake at the top of the drink when it settles.

THE SHIRLEY SPRITZ

Even when I was a kid, I think I was already figuring out how fun it is to pair drinks with dinner. I remember going out with my parents to a restaurant on Fridays and ordering a Shirley Temple to go with my meal. While there are recipes for "adult" Shirley Temples, these days I prefer my adult spin on it to be the Aperol Spritz. The bright red color and the carbonation are there, and they are just delicious. This recipe is not too far from the classic, but with a little less prosecco, more club soda, and more dilution from the small cubes or crushed ice, it drinks less boozy.

Small cubed ice or **crushed ice**, for serving
2 ounces (60 ml) **Aperol**
2 ounces (60 ml) **club soda**
2 ounces (60 ml) **prosecco**
1 **fresh orange slice or Dried Candied Orange Slice** (page 176)

Serves 1

Fill a large wine glass with ice. Pour in the Aperol first, then the club soda and prosecco. Pour gently, and stop pouring and then add more if you are getting too many bubbles. Stir gently for 5 to 10 seconds. Garnish with the orange slice.

> **CHEAT CODE:** Take some of your orange slices and put two slices on the glass, then add ice. The ice will hold the orange slices to the wall of the glass for a nice presentation.

CHERRY SNOW ANGEL

1 **large egg white**
2 ounces (30 ml) **gin**
½ ounce (15 ml) freshly squeezed **lime juice**
¼ ounce (8 ml) **Aperol**
¼ ounce (8 ml) **Maraschino cherry liqueur**
Crushed ice, for mixing
Few drops **aromatic bitters**

Serves 1

1. Pour the egg white into the shaker. Cover and dry shake (meaning, shake with no ice cubes) hard for 30 seconds to 1 minute, or until extremely frothy. After your dry shake, add the gin, lime juice, Aperol, and cherry liqueur, re-cover, and dry shake again for 30 seconds.

2. Now, it's time to add the ice. Fill the shaker with ice, cover, and shake for 30 seconds more. Strain into a chilled coupe glass.

> **CHEAT CODE:** You will know the drink is ready when the tin is ice cold.

3. The finisher is aromatic bitters. Carefully drop a few into the cocktail foam. Drag a toothpick through the bitters. For maximum razzle-dazzle, switch up where you drop the bitters and how you drag the toothpick for different designs.

I think egg white drinks scare some people off. But don't run. Doing a dry shake with the egg white agitates the egg white and breaks down the proteins. When done correctly, the egg white turns frothy and combines with the spirit for a creamy-textured drink. Nothing else can replicate that texture.

Gin, by nature, is one of the stronger spirits, and I think it can handle flavored additions better than many other spirits. This is a super fun way to introduce someone to gin, or if you're looking for something different from the standard gin martini.

ORANGE + CHERRY

2 ounces (60 ml) **100-proof whiskey**
½ ounce (15 ml) **Maraschino cherry liqueur**
1½ ounces (45 ml) freshly squeezed **orange juice**
3 dashes **sorghum bitters**
1 large **ice cube**
Orange twist, for garnish

Serves 1

The majority of whiskey- and bourbon-based cocktail recipes are constructed to let the whiskey speak and to accent the whiskey. This recipe, instead, is a fully flavored, fun drink without it being all whiskey. It has a fruit punch vibe. If you know someone who prefers a sweeter, bourbon-based cocktail, this is a great option for them even though it uses a higher-proof whiskey.

In a mixing glass, combine all the ingredients except the orange peel and stir for 30 seconds. Strain into a chilled whiskey tumbler with a fresh, large ice cube. While you can express the orange peel (twist and squeeze it over the cocktail), add it to the cocktail, and serve, I love flaming the orange oils instead. To do this, I use a kitchen torch to hit the edge of the peel for just a second before dropping it into the glass. With a bit of practice, you can also use a match, holding it between the orange peel and the drink, lighting the oils on their way to the glass.

By using sorghum bitters, you accent the flavor of the whiskey. They have two main notes: earthy and caramel. Because of the sweeter ingredients in this cocktail, you'll want the bitters to help with the contrasting flavor of the whiskey—so the drink isn't overly sweet.

STRAWBERRY OLD-FASHIONED, TWO WAYS

As I mention frequently, the Old-Fashioned is my go-to bourbon drink, and I love putting different spins on an otherwise classic cocktail. Strawberry is a wonderful flavor to add to an Old-Fashioned, and I have two ways to get the berry into the drink. First, you can add a puree. When you puree strawberries, the sugars break down and you end up with a jamlike texture that's great for mixing into drinks. The other option is to muddle the fruit. Muddling will break up the fruit but break down less sugar. If you are a purist and want a more bourbon-heavy drink, go muddled. If you want more of a mixed cocktail experience, go pureed. You can't miss with either.

¼ cup (38 g) **fresh strawberries**, hulled and halved, plus slices for garnish
2 ounces (60 ml) **simple syrup** or **Oleo** of choice (page 168)
2 ounces (60 ml) **100-proof bourbon whiskey**
8 dashes **Angostura bitters**
1 cup (120 g) **ice**

Serves 4

OLD-FASHIONED WITH STRAWBERRY PUREE

Place the strawberries and simple syrup in a thick glass. Blend using an immersion blender until you achieve a smooth puree. Transfer to a cocktail shaker and add the bourbon whiskey, bitters, and ice. Stir with a bar spoon for about 1 minute until the ingredients are well combined. Do not shake! If your shaker is metal, you will see frost form on the outside of the shaker. Strain the drink into four coupe glasses, catching the pureed strawberries in your strainer. Garnish each with a strawberry slice.

OLD-FASHIONED WITH MUDDLED STRAWBERRIES

In a cocktail shaker, muddle the strawberries until well mashed. Add the simple syrup, bourbon whiskey, bitters, and ice. Stir with a bar spoon for about 1 minute until the ingredients are well combined. Do not shake! If using a metal shaker, you will see frost form on the outside of the shaker. Strain the drink into four lowball glasses. Garnish each with a strawberry slice.

RESOURCES

APRON

I get asked where I got my apron almost daily. The two famous leather aprons, the signature call of duty and standard, are both made by Dalstrong (Dalstrong.com). They are 100 percent leather and the most durable I have ever used. They are also "big boy" friendly and don't look like a bib on me.

KNIVES

If you are buying a gift, I recommend Dalstrong (Dalstrong.com) knives. When I first started cooking, my first knife was a Dalstrong quantum series. Over time I started understanding steel hardness. And Dalstrong has a lot of options and different variations. You can have fourteen or fifteen chef's knives to choose from. So, if you're looking for something like a larger or smaller handle, you can find it.

My favorite Japanese knife is Miyabi and, for entry level, I do like Hexclad (Hexclad.com) as well; they are Damascus steel. My personal preference is a Hexclad chef's knife and cleaver.

If you know a bladesmith, you can also go custom.

PANS

Cuisinel
The underside of the lids on their Dutch ovens have points, so when you're baking bread, the lids help eliminate extra moisture, almost steaming the bread to get a great crust.

Hexclad
If you follow me on social media, I have explored safe versus nonsafe in this space and I feel comfortable with Hexclad—the design of the pan, overall durability, ease of cleaning, and its different applications, and how they hold up over time (and that includes the nonstick surface not wearing off as well as aesthetics). When it comes to kitchen tools, Hexclad is top tier. I have their salt and pepper mill, mixing bowls, and I use all their pans when I cook.

Lodge
(LodgeCastIron.com) I think everyone needs a 10-inch cast-iron skillet, minimum. Camp Chef (CampChef.com) also makes good cast iron.

SPICES

Spiceology (Spiceology.com): The reason I like Spiceology is that it's started by chefs. It's one of the few big spice companies still owned by the original founders. My favorite, Smoky Honey Habanero seasoning, is actually the first seasoning Pete Taylor put out. All of their seasonings are responsibly sourced, are made without additives, and I love the identity. I absolutely love their periodic table of spices, and I have an entire four-tier shelf in my kitchen filled with them, and I love how they look when displayed. They also have an affinity for stepping outside the box for what a standard seasoning is. Spiceology gives you a lot of variety while letting you try seasonings you may or may not grab in the grocery stores.

ACKNOWLEDGMENTS

Without God, who I am would not be possible. Continue to order my steps!

Mom and Dad, thank you for always being pillars of strength and SHOWING me how to love unconditionally. Your continued wisdom and support are huge reasons this book became reality.

Grandma, thank you for showing me how to cook with love every Sunday after church! I'll always be your pride and joy, your baby boy!

To my wife, Tee, thank you for supporting my dreams, no matter how big or crazy. I promise to give you the kitchen back, one day.

Ayanna, Elyse, Adrian, and Travis, my babies. Continue to unapologetically be yourselves. One of the greatest gifts God has given me has been the chance to be a father. Just know, wherever you are, Dad's got you if you need me. Those dreams, dream 'em big!

Special shout-out to my editor, Thom, who saw this vision first. I couldn't have picked a better teammate for my first book. Kelsey, thanks for making the photo shoots a blast.

To all my "one takers" on social media, thank you for your continued support. The community we have developed online has truly been special, and I am looking forward to growing it even bigger.

ABOUT THE AUTHOR

Bo Corley is a cooking creator who is passionate about great food and designing recipes that work for busy families. A former insurance company executive (and proud eighth- and ninth-grade oratory champion), Bo's journey with food started when he was a kid: exploring in the kitchen, family dinners, and Sunday dinners at his grandma's. After some time away from the kitchen for a corporate career, Bo found himself weighing close to 500 pounds (227 kg) and ready to take back control of his nutrition through cooking. He resolved to lose weight but still enjoy his meals. Eventually, he shared his chef-y takes on healthy meals online and Bo the Goat TV was born. In the years since, Bo has grown in many ways, including his journey with grilling/smoking and experimenting with cocktails. His current mission is to cook for his family and spread his love of cooking to as many people as possible. Bo's cooking videos and recipes have frequently gone viral and been featured everywhere from various TV morning shows to *BuzzFeed Tasty* to the *New York Post*. Find him online across social media as @bothegoattv.

INDEX

Note: Page references in *italics* indicate photographs.